Be Bolder Growin' Older

Overcoming the Temptations of Old Age

by

Bruce Leiter

Author of *Doubtbusters! God Is My Shrink!*

Be Bolder Growin' Older

CrossLink Publishing
www.crosslinkpublishing.com

Copyright, © 2013 Bruce Leiter

All rights reserved. No part of this book may be reproduced in any form, except for brief quotations in reviews, without the written permission of the author.

Printed in the United States of America. All rights reserved under International Copyright Law.

ISBN 978-1-936746-76-7

Library of Congress Number: 2013949377

Scripture quotations are taken from the Holy Bible, NEW INTERNATIONAL VERSION®. Copyright © 1973, 1978, 1984, 2011 by Biblica, Inc. Used by permission. All rights reserved worldwide.

Full permission given by Keith Drury for use of his Web article "Ten Temptations of Old Age."

Seven Essential Tips for Reading
Be Bolder Growin' Older

Tip Number One: When I saw Keith Drury's Internet article "Ten Temptations of Old Age," I asked him for his permission to use it in my book. He gave me his full permission. The book, patterned on his discovery of ten temptations through research with older people, has ten chapters with two parts each. <u>All ten chapters move you from a description of the Bible's view of those sins toward new biblical qualities that God can give us</u> to replace those temptations to sin, through victorious prayers, words, and actions.

Tip Number Two: Throughout the ten chapters about the ten temptations of old age are <u>steps of application</u>, prayer-word-and-action ways that we can "be bolder growin' older" to make progress in Jesus' victory over those sins.

Tip Number Three: Those steps take us on a <u>joyful journey with Jesus</u> toward his final goal for our lives.

Tip Number Four: In front of each step are <u>discussion questions for small groups and Bible studies</u>. A <u>free leader's discussion guide</u> is available at my e-mail <u>bolder-older@gmx.com</u>.

Tip Number Five: This book contrasts the <u>Bible's old and new situations</u>, the latter of which is our goal now.

Tip Number Six: This book is a <u>devotional Bible study</u> for individual readers and for group discussion.

Tip Number Seven: Following is the <u>overview of the book with its chapters and steps</u> for your benefit:

Chapter One: *From* our old self-centeredness *to* our new God-centeredness 1

<u>One Step on Our Journey with Jesus</u>: Three suggested daily prayers follow: Praise your Creator for his power in making you his special creature. Admit the fact that you have fallen with Adam to shame with hope. Confess your sins daily as Jesus showed us in the Lord's Prayer.

<u>One Step on Our Journey with Jesus:</u> Pray for God the Father's power through Jesus by the Holy Spirit to repent of your self-centeredness, and pray constantly to overcome that proud self-dependence and to rely on him to run your life rather than you. "Be bolder" by expressing openly and persistently in prayer any anger or anxiety that you have about losses in your life until God gives you his permanent peace.

<u>One Step on Our Journey with Jesus:</u> Admit and confess persistently your completely-guilty imperfection before God and seek the inner peace that reflects Jesus' gift of outer peace with our Judge.

<u>One Step On Our Journey with Jesus:</u> Admit and accept the fact that you cannot in any way earn God's acceptance and love on your own, because you are incapable of pleasing God in your own power. Confess daily your inability to please him in your own strength, and ask him for his power through Jesus' victory by the Spirit's presence to live for him.

Chapter Two: *From* Old Feelings of Worthlessness *to* New Feelings of Worth: 49

One Step on Our Journey with Jesus: Resolve to give your thought-life to God to pray to God against the devil and for God's victory in your life and in the lives of people you know. Also, give your thoughts to praising the 3-in-1 God's greatness.

One Step on Our Journey with Jesus: If you haven't already accepted Jesus Christ's life, death, and resurrection as God's only way for you to be rescued, ask him for his free gift of new birth. If you have, praise him daily for his amazing gift of the new birth by his grace (free acceptance). "Be bolder growin' older" in prayer for endurance in life's struggles as you approach and endure old age.

Chapter Three: *From* old selfish use of money *to* new generosity 61

One Step on Our Journey with Jesus: Decide to plan a budget that puts giving at least ten percent of your income to spiritual causes first, paying off your debts second, and spending third in using the income with which God has blessed you. Always remember that it's God's income, not yours. You only manage it for him.

Chapter Four: *From* old giving up on life *to* new giving in to God ...75

One Step on Our Journey with Jesus: "Be bolder growin' older" by persistently asking God to show you the worthwhile activities in which he wants you to be involved until he shows you his will. Then, do them prayerfully to honor him.

Chapter Five: *From* feeling abandoned *to* feeling God's powerful presence 93

One Step on Our Journey with Jesus: Let yourself cry persistently and freely in private as you express your loneliness, anger, feeling of abandonment, or other feelings openly and honestly to God. Resolve by God's grace to ask for his guidance to be his agent of blessing in other people's lives.

Chapter Six: *From* bitterness *to* permanent peace about life 111

One Step on Our Journey with Jesus: If you suspect that you might have some unresolved anger or bitterness but can't remember what the original cause might be, get psychological help to discover what you are *really* angry about. Then, express and confess your anger persistently in prayer until God gives you his peace.

One Step on Our Journey with Jesus: Examine your life with psychological help, if necessary, for any anger or bitterness about past losses or reverses. Pray perseveringly private prayers that openly express your anger and anxiety about past and present losses and other people's unloving actions. Persist in prayer asking for God's promised, permanent peace until he gives it to you.

Chapter Seven: *From* old despair *toward* new integrity 131

One Step on Our Journey with Jesus: Persistently confess all of your sinfulness to God in prayer until he gives you peace about your far-from-perfect past. Experience his resulting gift of peace that is focused on him as your peace-giver instead of despair as you look at your life.

One Step On Our Journey with Jesus: Devote your prayers to include joyful praise for God's free gift of Jesus' perfection in your life as a believer.

Chapter Eight: *From* old doubt *to* new confidence in the God of the Bible 141

One Step on Our Journey with Jesus: Confess in prayer the human-experience thinking, feeling, and deciding that still remain in your life, and pray persistently that God's life and experience may fill your life as you read the Bible.

One Step on Our Journey with Jesus: Ask God in persistent prayer to use the victory of Jesus' life, death, and resurrection to give you spiritual progress in accomplishing his goals for your middle and/or old age. Claim Jesus' victory for you to make you more joyful, prayerful, and thankful.

Chapter Nine: *From* old losing our faith *to* new growing in our faith 153

One Step on Our Journey with Jesus: If you have questions about God's involvement in your life and the universe, confess that you have let your human experience color your thinking. Ask God to give you his perspective through his Word and other Christians.

One Step on Our Journey with Jesus: Challenge yourself to read, meditate on, and/or memorize three of the Hebrews 12 and 13 commandments every day for twelve days. Pray daily for Jesus' triumph to give you his Holy

Spirit to put them into practice. Reread this book at some point for insights into God's Word that you missed the first time, and pray to God for his strength to follow Jesus more and more.

Chapter Ten: *From* morbid fixation on death *to* hopeful assurance about life beyond death... 173

<u>One Step on Our Journey with Jesus:</u> Recall people's unloving actions and your life's losses. "Be bolder growin' older" by praying laments privately like Psalms 39 and 88. Persistently tell God honestly and openly with tears the anger and/or anxiety that you feel about those events in your life. At the same time, persistently confess your selfishness in wanting your own loss-free plan for your life rather than God's plan allowing those losses.

<u>One Step on Our Journey with Jesus:</u> Fill your mind with praise for the hope of our final resurrection and our future entrance in the new, perfected universe.

<u>One Step on Our Journey with Jesus:</u> Ask God for his gifts of courage and words to enable you to repair any broken relationships with family members or other people from whom you are estranged. Ask God also to strengthen your relationship with him so that it's the most important covenant relationship in your life. Then, seek to be God's agent of blessing to the people around you.

<u>One Step on Our Journey with Jesus:</u> Thank the Lord in your prayers that our future as believers is secure because of Jesus' life, death, and resurrection. Express your gratitude in your daily life for the tangible hope that he has given you.

<u>One Step on Our Journey with Jesus:</u> In your prayers, praise God the Father for his perfect justice (his "guilty" verdict) that he gave to Jesus in our place. Praise Jesus for his perfect substitution for us on the cross taking on himself our Father's just anger against our sins. Praise the Holy Spirit for giving us faith and the new birth to live for the one eternal God in his strength, not our own. Praise him as your one true God.

<u>The Final Step on Our Journey with Jesus:</u> Give up by God's grace your reliance on earthly things and people for satisfaction and meaning. Instead, focus your hope on the God of the Bible to run the race humbly, boldly, and prayerfully. Ask him to make you his agent of blessing to other people. Pray persistently for his power to persevere on the path toward perfection.

ACKNOWLEDGMENTS

I acknowledge the help of my wonderful wife, Winnie, without whose assistance this book would be much less effective. Of course, I give my hearty thanks to Keith Drury, who gave his generous, full permission for me to use his Internet article "Ten Temptations of Old Age." Also, I give my heartfelt thanks to Rick Bates and the fine folks at CrossLink Publishing for editing and publishing this devotional Bible study. Finally, I give my deepest, most profound thanks to the only true God of the Bible, who blessed me with my writing career as a retired pastor and guided this book's research, writing, and publication.

Bruce Leiter the Writer.

Be Bolder Growin' Older: Overcoming the Temptations of Old Age

```
      As
      we                              move...
    travel                              to
      on                              Jesus
    Jesus'                           through
    journey                           power
    toward                             his
      our                              us
     final                            gives
       goal,     God
```

Chapter One: *From* our old self-centeredness *to* our new God-centeredness

1. <u>From our old self-centeredness:</u>

Credit where credit is due

I am indebted to Keith Drury for his insightful article "The Temptations of Old Age" (http://www.drurywriting.com/keith/sins.of.old.age.htm), which I used with his full permission as background for the ten chapters of this book. However, my book is a devotional Bible study that emphasizes how we can make progress in overcoming the sins of old age as they tempt us.

Thus, the question arises, how can we overcome the temptations of old age? When Keith Drury asked many older adults about their lives, he discovered ten of their temptations to sin. This book, which is indebted to his insights, explores how God can enable us to overcome those sinful temptations, according to God's Word, the Bible.

Keith states, "While we expect sainthood from the aged, sin crouches at the door through all stages of life." His point is that older people's sins take a different form from those of younger people but are nonetheless just as real.

God wants us to "be bolder growin' older" on our tremendous trip toward our final bliss by overcoming the temptations that often weigh older people down.

The beginning sentence after the book's title explained

The strange sentence above that descends and then ascends, ending with chapter one's title, reads as follows: *As we travel on Jesus' journey toward our final goal, God gives us his power through Jesus to move...*from *our old self-centeredness* to *our new God-centeredness.* That sentence goes down and up to illustrate our need to humble ourselves from our high position of sinful pride, in which we are born, to ascend in God's strength as we become more and more like Jesus. I call that spiritual process in all true Christians the parabola of humility in chapter one, part two. It also summarizes this book during our life-trip in Jesus' victory.

The first sentence and this book's pattern follows the one in James 4:10, "Humble yourselves before the Lord, and he will lift you up."

This book as our journey following twenty-four steps with Jesus toward our final destiny

This book is a trip toward believers' final destination with twenty-four steps along the way through ten chapters describing how we can progress from our old sins to God's new qualities that he wants to increase in us. Come with me on our Road, Jesus, to God's future new world. As we journey through these ten besetting sins with Jesus as our Path to God the Father, we will examine from the Bible how God can make us "bolder growin' older" to overcome them in his power. He can enable us to move our lives from the old situation with which we were born to the new experience that God plans for all believers.

This book as a description of the old and new situations in the Bible

The Bible is full of references to our old lives, as well as the 3-in-1 God's calls to the new lives he wants to give us. That transformation in our lives can only take place in his strength through Jesus' victory by the Holy Spirit's power. It happens through faith in the one, only true God by his grace shown through Jesus' life, death, and resurrection. They are amazing events that enable us to move from our old natures more and more to our new natures that he has given us.

The need for our journey from self-centeredness toward God-centeredness

Chuck Swindoll illustrates our dilemma of getting older in "How to Know You're Getting Older," *Strengthening Our Grip*, page 128:

> Everything hurts, and what doesn't hurt, doesn't work!
> You feel like the night before, and you haven't been anywhere!
> You sit in a rocking chair and can't get it going!
> Your knees buckle and your belt won't!
> Dialing long distance wears you out!
> The little gray-haired lady you help across the street is your wife!
> You sink your teeth into a steak, and they stay there!
> When you wake up in the morning, your waterbed has sprung a leak. Then you realize that you don't have a waterbed!
> As you watch a pretty girl go by, your pacemaker makes the garage door go up!
> You're old when you know all the answers, but no one asks you the questions!
> You're old when you decide to procrastinate, but you never get around to it!

These exaggerated, humorous observations point up the fact that our older years do not always come out the way we had imagined them when we were younger. The result is that we are often tempted to sin against God, who allows us to struggle during our last decades of life.

The first temptation to sin, human pride

Therefore, let's begin our journey toward God's spiritual improvement. Keith Drury's first sinful temptation is self-centeredness, a quality with which all of us are conceived and born. It is the central feature of our sinful natures and is present throughout our lives. In fact, sin is self-centeredness.

However, often, when we grow older, selfishness becomes more prominent, since we have more time and freedom to live a self-centered life. Retired older people demonstrate their selfishness in different ways. Some spend freely for themselves the money they have accumulated; while others hold on to it without benefiting themselves, their families, or worthy causes for fear of running out of their wealth because of possible nursing home expenses.

Initially, we must discover how the old self-centeredness in all of us began in order to find out how we can progress to God-centeredness. In this way, we have the sad duty to find out the quicksand depths into which humanity sank in their rebellion against their Maker. Then, we can discover the dizzying heights of God-centeredness to which he lifts his own loved ones in order to increase abundantly the generous thankfulness of our lives on our trip toward God's final deliverance.

We begin in the book of beginnings, Genesis. In chapter one, God creates every object and all living beings "very good." Moses' inspired point in that chapter is that the all-powerful Creator, who is separate from his handiwork, speaks his creative words to bring into being the complex, amazingly-designed universe, as well as humans as its perfect rulers under him.

Then, Moses gives more details in Genesis chapter two by showing God's life-giving work. He describes God's special creation of Adam out of the dirt as his only living being with a soul. All of God's creation is still "very good" at this point.

However, it is from that pinnacle of perfection, while the human couple effortlessly garden in God's created paradise, that the human race's perfection comes to a screeching halt. Instead of spending their lives in obedient thankfulness, Adam and Eve willfully and rebelliously plunge precipitously into the depths of deceit and despair. The meaning of the dastardly deed isn't merely that they consume a forbidden fruit, but their sinful actions show that they want to be equal with God. They decide to run their own lives as separate people trying to be equal with him. Their action is treason!

When we do our daily tasks without consulting God in prayer, our actions are similarly treasonous.

From the heights of heavenly happiness to the depths of despair and destruction, Adam as the head of humanity falls along with his suitable helper, Eve. Moreover, God rightly punishes Satan, in the guise of the serpent's guile, along with Adam and Eve, whose self-centeredness clearly shows up in their blame-game perpetrated against each other and against God (3:8-13).

Hope in the middle of despair

However, in the middle of God's pronounced curses on the treacherous, treasonous trio comes a glimmer of hope (3:15) that he delivers, interestingly, as part of his just curse on the serpent: "And I will put enmity between you and the woman, and between your offspring and hers; he will crush your head, and you will strike his heel." The Hebrew word translated "offspring" means humankind collectively with a single human being as its head ("he"), according to Brown, Driver, and Briggs' *Hebrew and English Lexicon of the Old Testament* (Oxford, 1959), page 282. In other words, a male head of the human race will achieve a crushing victory over Satan, who will hit him with a glancing blow; he represents all humans in that convincing win.

Guess who that Winner is and who can be winners with him. You guess right. Jesus, the Messiah, reverses the curse for us who accept his life, death, and resurrection as our divine-human Winner, the Head of the church. He crushes Satan's head by his death on the cross, though it appears as though the Evil One wins. Note Galatians 3:13a: "Christ redeemed us from the curse of the law by becoming a curse for us ..." on the cursed criminal's cross. What a perfect, divine-human Pinch-Hitter he is! He sets us free through his own death by taking the punishment that we deserve and, eventually, transfers his perfection to all true believers!

My point is that in the middle of the dark punishmentphase of Adam's sinful treason, the God of grace (free acceptance) offers a way out through the future Messiah's dramatic reversal of our rebellion. That same God provides a blip of tunnel light that results in the coming of the Light of the world. He lives and dies for the world and, more definitely, for his own loved, adopted brothers and sisters.

I've experienced human fallenness with more than twenty-five years of physical pain. God provides ways to get relief, peace about it, and grace to live with it. However, pain is always present in my body the way sin is always present in our lives.

Bible Discussion Questions:

1. Read Genesis 1. How have you experienced amazement about God's creation recently? How did his divine power shine through his world to you in that encounter? How is that same part of God's creation also fallen or imperfect? Explain.
2. Read Genesis 2. In your own words, what is Adam and Eve's life like in the Garden of Eden? What evidence of humility is shown

by Adam's creation from dirt? How can we gain God's power to replace pride with humility before our great Creator? Explain.
3. Read Genesis 3. What untruths and half-truths does Satan tell Eve to tempt her? Define sin. How does it show up in our lives? Give examples from the world around you.
4. Summarize the curses (punishments) that God gives to Satan, Adam, and Eve. What examples of the curse do you see in people's lives and the world around you?
5. What glimmer of hope does God give in the middle of the curses (Genesis 3:15)? How can we gain relief from the curse's results? How have you experienced Jesus' victory over the curse described in Galatians 3:13? How can we experience more of God's deliverance?

* * *

One Step on Our Journey with Jesus: **Three suggested daily prayers follow: Praise your Creator for his power in making you as his special creature. Admit the fact that you have fallen with Adam to shame with hope. Confess your sins daily as Jesus showed us in the Lord's Prayer.**

* * *

Bruce Leiter

Personal rebellion

In 1960, I attended Calvin College with God's call to be a pastor two years after he made me a true believer. However, the requirement at that time, a Greek major, seemed like climbing Mount Everest to me. As a result, I rebelled the same way Jonah ran away from God's call for him to preach in Nineveh, Israel's archrival. I decided, instead, to major in and teach English after considering three other majors. Thus, I ran away from God's call to preach by becoming a teacher. My self-centered rebellion prevented me from praying for God's guidance.

An unknown writer made the following observation, "Our pastor called the other day and told my wife, Helen, that she should start thinking about the hereafter. 'Oh, I do, I do,' Helen told him. 'No matter where I am, I ask myself, What am I here after?'" Memory problems often come with old age and can cause frustration.

I also had a "memory problem" by "forgetting" God's call to be a pastor. Remembering in the Bible is more than a mere mental exercise, it also involves obeying the God that we remember.

However, Adam and Eve's plunge into sin causes our many imperfections.

Not only are we humans fallen with Adam like an empty titanium balloon from the glorious perfection of underrulers with God over his creation, but we also lift ourselves up from perfect humility under God's loving rule in order to gain equal status with God, even though we are mere creatures. The gall of the human race is our attempt to raise ourselves to our all-powerful Maker's awesomely-high level! That heavy hubris rather than heavenly humility is at the center of our sinful self-centeredness in climbing high and lifting ourselves up as our own rulers instead of submitting to the only true, divine Ruler, who made us. Lifting ourselves up in pride is our downfall!

Thus, planning our lives in self-centeredness, as I did during my teaching and sales management careers rather than asking God for his guidance, is an example of old age's sins. The divine irony is that God guided me even as I rebelled against his call to the ministry.

Humans' parabola of pride

I call the self-raising of the human race the parabola of pride, of which I am guilty. A parabola in mathematics is a curved line that arches like the arch in St. Louis, Missouri, high above a line and then returns to the same line at a different place. It can also dip in a downward arch, depending on which equation creates it. (You can consult a mathematician for more details.)

We humans in Adam have arched high by trying to reach God's level in our parabola of pride in order to run our own lives. Actually, it's really Satan controlling our plans if we have not trusted in Jesus to guide them.

Several examples of this parabola in the Bible follow.

For example, Adam starts out perfect, like God, but far from divine. "So God created human beings in his own image, in the image of God he created them; male and female he created them" (Genesis 1:27). Moses' inspired excitement in that verse shows as he enthusiastically repeats the word "create" three times. He, at the same time, emphasizes the humility of created humans under their all-powerful, separate Creator.

Then, in chapter two, Moses puts Adam a little above the level of dirt—that's humility!—from which he came (verse 7). His very life was God's gift of grace (free acceptance). On the other hand, the LORD graciously lifts him to the role of ruler over the earth under the royal Ruler's rule. Thus, the emphatic focus falls on Adam's humble beginnings and his gardening career (verse 15). Later in the same chapter, God makes Eve from Adam's side (verses 21 and 22), another humble origin, as his assistant gardener.

Therefore, God's will for our daily tasks is that we seek his guidance and direction in caring for his creation, whether it means cleaning and taking care of our houses--even the bathroom!--or being active in our church.

Our first human ancestors, in their parabola of pride, lose their cushy, perfect situation by thinking that they know best how to run their lives apart from their benevolent Creator's loving will. Their *seemingly*-unimportant grab at power (Genesis 3:5, 6) plunges them from their perfectly humble position to the heights and depths of pride, resulting in their humiliating exile from God's garden of grace.

Thus, God deflates their rebellious parabola of pride. Humiliating, self-centered pride produces the curse of the depth of defeat. We rebellious humans virtually always turn God's truth on its head by calling good evil. We also pronounce evil good.

God's contrast of his divine nature with human nature

As we continue our examination of human self-centeredness, we find that Isaiah 40:15, 17, 21, 22 contrasts humbled humanity with the awesome grandeur of our Creator God: "Surely the nations are like a drop in a bucket; they are regarded as dust on scales; he weighs the islands as though they were fine dust.... Before him all the nations are as nothing; they are regarded by him as worthless and less than nothing.... Do you not know? Have you not heard? Has it not been told you from the beginning? Have you not understood since the earth was founded? He sits enthroned above the circle of the earth, and its people are like grasshoppers. He stretches out the heavens like a canopy and spreads them out like a tent to live in." God inspires Isaiah to compare us who think that we're big stuff to a water drop, dust, Adam-stuff (verse 15), and nothing (verse 17). Talk about knocking us humans down a peg!

Then, after God rightly ridicules meaningless idol worship, he contrasts his regal position "above the circle of the earth" with his lowly human grasshoppers (verse 22). He can sweep humanity's high, planted positions away as with a desert tornado (verse 23). God's point is that he rules the universe and that we do not, especially our lives.

On the other hand, it's our parabola of pride that keeps us human insects reliant on ourselves and other humans rather than on our Creator-God.

Our pride also denies or tries to escape growing older and dying. However, the Bible helps us face and find Jesus' victory over old age's sins.

Our world talks about the need for self-confidence and a positive self-image. However, such comments all revolve around self. We need to shift our focus from ourselves in self-confidence to a God-confidence that centers on our amazing Creator-Rescuer God as the source of our lives' strength and abilities!

Our discovery of the depths of humiliating human hubris continues with 2 Chronicles 26. Even Uzziah, king of Judah, who is described as doing "right in the eyes of the LORD" (verse 5), lifts himself in pride. "God gave him success..." when "he sought the LORD" (verse 5b). However, "after Uzziah became powerful, his pride led to his downfall. He was unfaithful to the LORD..." by trying to burn incense in the temple, a decidedly-priestly task. When he becomes angry at the priests who confront him with his sinful disobedience, the LORD allows him to be afflicted with lifelong leprosy (verses 16-21), thus making him unclean in God's sight. When we lift ourselves to a level beyond our proper place in a parabola of pride, such actions result in eventual, permanent punishment.

God's redirection

You probably wonder what happened to my self-centered rebellion. Well, I was very restless as I taught English for eight years in five schools. In the last year of my teaching career, our second son, Keith, died from leukemia. During the almost-three years of his sickness, a very traumatic time in our lives, my wife and I came down with hepatitis and suffered with Keith through all of his spinal taps, struggles, and shots.

In spite of our great stress, God changed my heart to seek prayerfully his will for my vocational life rather than my own. After three years as a sales manager, I sensed God's overwhelming, renewed call to the ministry. Thus, with a wife, no job, and three children, I returned to school to become a pastor. Amazingly, God took care of our needs.

Bible Discussion Questions:

1. Pick three of the following passages to discuss: 1 Corinthians 11:3; Genesis 3; Isaiah 40:15-24; Leviticus 26:13-39; 2 Chronicles 26; 2 Chronicles 32:24-26. How do these passages illustrate the humanly-sinful parabola of pride? How has God humbled you through his Word and circumstances that he has allowed in your life? How can we overcome self-centeredness in old age?

2. How has God humbled you through his Word and circumstances that he has allowed in your life? How can we overcome self-centeredness in old age? Explain.

* * *

One Step on Our Journey with Jesus: Pray for God the Father's power through Jesus by the Holy Spirit to repent of your self-centeredness, and pray constantly to overcome that proud self-dependence and to rely on him to run your life rather than you. Surrender your life to Jesus' leadership.

* * *

Dealing with proud, selfish frustration

Part of my self-centeredness like the rest of humanity is occasional frustration when life doesn't go my way. I pray that God will replace it with submission to his plan. For example, I lost a revision of this book and got frustrated when my computer failed to work right. God led me to express and confess my frustration in prayer, and I continue to pray for submission to God's permitted plan. I see now that my book became much better through several revisions.

Another part of the good that God brought out of that situation was a new, dependable computer that I pray that he will keep working well as his tool in his hands over my hands.

Another example of God's punishment of human pride is Nebuchadnezzar's experience in Daniel 4. Daniel interprets the dream of the king of Babylon about a large tree that is cut down. God then fulfills that dream in the king's life as follows: "All this happened to King Nebuchadnezzar. Twelve months later, as the king was walking on the roof of the royal palace of Babylon, he said, 'Is not this the great Babylon I have built as the royal residence, by my mighty power and for the glory of my majesty?' Even as the words were on his lips, a voice came from heaven, 'This is what is decreed for you, King Nebuchadnezzar: Your royal authority has been taken from you. You will be driven away from people and will live with wild animals; you will eat grass like the ox. Seven times will pass for you until you acknowledge that the Most High is sovereign over the kingdoms on earth and gives them to anyone he wishes.'"

Of course, God immediately fulfills his prediction in the dream. Nebuchadnezzar's insanity lasts until the king humbles himself before the Ruler of the universe. Sadly, we as the human race are also doomed to receive punishment unless we learn not to repeat Nebuchadnezzar's pride. We proud humans need to flee, instead, to the Messiah-Rescuer with repentant, changed hearts.

As Solomon, who gathers many inspired proverbs but doesn't always follow his own advice in his daily life—a distinctly human trait—writes in Proverbs 16:18, 19: "Pride goes before destruction, a haughty spirit before a fall. Better to be lowly in spirit along with the oppressed than to share plunder with the proud." Notice that it does not directly say, "Pride goes before a fall," as the popular saying goes. I guess that it's also a human trait to avoid any thought of "destruction."

Sadly, the pattern of our inborn habit of lifting ourselves up to run our own lives instead of letting God guide us, a self-destructive path that Adam began, continues throughout the Bible and into the present.

The next step on our trip toward understanding the full sweep of the Bible's promise of victory takes us to Luke chapter nine. Jesus sends his twelve disciples to preach the good news and heal people (verses 1-6). Notice that the disciples have to learn full, humble dependence on God for their daily needs (verse 3).

The same lesson for the disciples and for us is partly involved in Christ's feeding of five thousand men along with their wives and children (verses 10-17). Always remember that Jesus pointedly tells his followers, "You give them something to eat" (verse 13a) and then teaches them a vivid illustration of how they are to feed that group as big as a good-sized town. His point is their need for full dependence on the Creator of all things, including his gifts of bread and fish.

Jesus' nonhuman teaching

In that same chapter, Peter, the usual spokesperson of Jesus' followers, boldly professes that their Leader is the Messiah (Anointed Ruler—verse 20).

However, Jesus follows Peter's public profession with a prediction of his suffering, death, and resurrection—three events that were foreign territory for the Jews of that day in their thinking about the coming messianic Ruler. They, instead, hoped for a political Messiah who would boot the iron-fisted Roman occupiers out of their land and set up his own rule on earth. Predictably, Jesus' description of his willing submission to suffering, his perfect humiliation, goes into one orifice of the disciples and out of another one without registering.

Then, Jesus illustrates for his followers the humble journey that all of his disciples, his disciplined followers, must follow as the parabola of humility that is the opposite of humans' parabola of pride. He upsets all human wisdom by stating, "All who want to be my disciples must deny themselves and take up their cross daily and follow me" (verse 23).

Thus, Jesus' way is the opposite of the human race's puffed-up path. Our culture raises us to embrace instead of deny ourselves, to avoid at all costs any kind of cross or suffering, and to ignore or reject dependence on God. The Bible has to be God's gift because no human mind could have come up with such nonhuman thinking.

Jesus' lessons in contrast to usual human thinking

In Luke 9:51, a turning point takes place as Jesus decides to take his journey to heaven (verse 51) by way of suffering, death, and resurrection in Jerusalem in order to accomplish God's removal of our guilt and his gift of new life. As the Messiah's advance men enter a Samaritan village to make preparations for the disciples' and Jesus' stay for the night, "the people did not welcome him, because he was heading for Jerusalem" (verse 53). In James' and John's extreme response, they propose to Jesus a violently-destructive solution, "Lord, do you want us to call fire down from heaven to destroy them?" (verse 54). Jesus simply rebukes them. "Might makes right" doesn't cut it with our Creator-Rescuer-Ruler.

Remember that two of Satan's temptations in Luke 4:1-13 are violent ones. In effect, he calls Jesus to zap the stones into bread and to swan-dive off the Jerusalem temple to demonstrate that he is the Son of God.

In addition, call to mind Christ's lesson of the two swords in the upper room and the Garden of Gethsemane (Luke 22:35-51). As he and his disciples prepare to depart from the upper room, Jesus curiously tells his followers to take two swords along to the garden. However, he then heals the ear of the high priest's servant when Peter rashly uses one of the swords during Jesus' arrest. It is a lesson that the disciples are not to use violence to advance Jesus' kingdom.

In addition, when Pilate examines Jesus, our divine-human Rescuer responds, "My kingdom is not of this world. If it were, my servants would fight to prevent my arrest by the Jews. My kingdom is from another place" (John 18:36).

Sadly, the church, especially during the Middle Ages and other times, has not followed Jesus' teachings that our "weapons" and our enemies are spiritual, not earthly ones (see Ephesians 6:10-20). God is the Judge, we aren't. Many Muslims hold long-standing grudges against the West because of our warfare against their ancestors during the Crusades, which were a horrible mistake.

Also, the exercise of human power-politics to get our way in the church is completely out of place. Human pride says that we have to defend our honor by getting our way. Even older people can be guilty of wanting the church to act their way.

However, Jesus and Paul have a different, divinely-inspired message about a divine Judge who will straighten everything out at the last day with guilty and not-guilty verdicts of all people. The intriguing discovery that we need to make is how to receive the second pronouncement instead of the first one, with which we are born.

Furthermore, as we discuss our lifting ourselves up in a coup to wrest the rule of the universe and our lives from the rightful Ruler of all, we examine the Parable of the Pharisee and the Tax Collector in Luke 18:9-14. The contrast can't be greater between the proud, pompous Pharisee, who leads an outwardly virtuous life that is admirable in every respect but who is caught in his own parabola of pride. Because of his pride, he heaps condescending disdain on the bent-over, evil sinner—also present in the temple—who legally cheats people out of their money on behalf of the evil Roman invader-occupiers of the Jews' Promised Land.

Often, we justify our pride in spending our old age the way we want to do by imagining that we are, after all, good people who deserve a little fun. We notice the same pattern that we have seen throughout the Bible that also infects the pious Pharisees, who are the most thoroughly-moral and biblically-sound people, at least publicly, of all God's people at that time. The trouble with squeaky-clean, public righteousness is that pride often rears its ugly face, brags about its "spiritual accomplishments," and looks down on other dastardly-dirty and doctrinally-deficient people.

Listen to the self-righteous, religiously-conservative man in his prayer, "God, *I* thank you that *I* am not like other people—robbers, evildoers, adulterers—or even like this tax collector. *I* fast twice a week and give a tenth of all *I* get" (Luke 18:11, 12). It isn't the Pharisee's posture of standing that Jesus condemns here, but he says that this "upright" man went home unjustified before God the Judge (verse 14). No, the self-absorbed inner-sinner refers to God once and to himself five times in his proud prayer, thus showing his true nature by his self-justification.

On the other hand, the broken, repentant tax collector, who is genuinely sorrowful about his sins, goes home God-justified.

Notice in verse 14b a pattern that Jesus, Peter, and James point out in the New Testament: "For all those who exalt themselves will be humbled, and those who humble themselves will be exalted" (Luke 18:14b). See also James 4:7-10. In addition, Peter teaches the second part of Jesus' saying in 1 Peter 5:5-7.

At this point, though, we must fix our attention on the first observation of Jesus. Furthermore, we have seen that the whole human race, after Adam's fall, has attempted to usurp the rule of God's universe, especially in our own lives, no matter how "good" our outward lives are.

The result in old age is that we can often be angry at God for allowing, not causing, the changes that occur in our lives as our bodies wear out. Often, we can be angry without knowing it.

Our expectations and the reality of growing older

The differences between our expectations and the reality of old age are illustrated by the following comical observations:
You know that you are old when:

>The gleam in your eye is the sunshine hitting your glasses.
>Your little black book contains only names ending in "M.D."
>You get winded playing chess.
>Your children look middle-aged.
>You finally reach the top of the ladder only to find it leaning against the wrong wall.
>You join a health club but don't go.
>Your mind makes contracts your body can't meet.
>You look forward to a dull evening.
>You walk with your head held high, trying to get used to your trifocals.
>You just can't stand people who are intolerant.

> The best part of the day is over when your alarm clock goes off.
> You burn the midnight oil after 9:00 P.M.
> Your back goes out more than you do. (source unknown)

God's grace to Noah and Abraham in an evil world

The next pause on our trip through old age toward our final triumph is a catastrophic one. The description of the universal flood is one of the saddest events in the Bible, second only in my eyes to the kangaroo courts and mistrials that send Jesus to an unjust, suffocating death. God's just punishment is not only for wicked human actions but also for the widespread, human, inner selfism that climbs the parabola of pride.

"The LORD [Yahweh] saw how great the wickedness of the human race had become on the earth, and that every inclination of the human heart was only evil all the time. The LORD was grieved that he had made human beings on the earth, and his heart was filled with pain" (Genesis 6:5, 6).

We see that God grieves over humans' pride-parabola and resolves to bring his judgment on them. Yet, his grace (free acceptance) is clear as he patiently waits for 120 years to give humans many opportunities to change their ways until he rescues believing, blameless Noah and his family. Noah certainly isn't perfect (Genesis 9:20-23) but is genuinely, blamelessly committed to the only true God as "a preacher of righteousness" (2 Peter 2:5).

God also demonstrates his universal grace after the flood with his covenant promise, shown by the rainbow, that he will never again send a universal flood on the earth to wipe out all life (Genesis 9:8-17). Oh, how full of patience and grace is our compassionate Creator, and how ungrateful are many humans!

The saga of the human parabola of pride that contrasts starkly with God's patient grace is also shown by the human hubris of the Tower of Babel (Genesis 11:1-8), where the just Judge of the universe has every right to strike people's pride with an instant death penalty. Instead, he confuses their languages.

Another important example is Genesis chapter twelve, where the LORD calls Abram to move again. That action describes an important turning point on our ongoing trip toward our final victory. He, his father, and their families have moved once already from Ur of the Chaldeans near present-day Kuwait as "southerners" to somewhere near the northwest corner of present-day Iraq on their way to Canaan to their southwest. In between, they settle in Haran in what is called Mesopotamia. After Abram's father, Terah, dies, somehow God renews his promises to our childless hero, whose name means "father."

The LORD's promises to Abram that a great nation will descend from him and that God will bless all nations through him are mind-boggling, especially since he is already seventy-five years old. Of course, the great and only God is certainly mind-boggling, isn't he?

How obedient would we have been in Abram's sandals? God says "Go" and Abram goes! That kind of submission, akin to Noah's construction project on dry ground, only happens because God enables him to make a leap of trust in him.

Twenty-four years later, in Genesis chapters 17 and 18, God shows his grace by repeating to Abraham and Sarah his plan to give them a son within a year when they will be 100 and 90 years old, respectively, as their natural-born heir.

Abraham's bold humility

Then, in chapter 18, Abraham overhears the LORD repeating his plans for Abraham and commenting on the wicked cities of the Jordan River Valley, Sodom and Gomorrah: "The outcry against Sodom and Gomorrah is so great and their sin so grievous that I will go down and see if what they have done is as bad as the outcry that has reached me. If not, I will know" (Genesis 18:20). God's solo speech is a test for Abraham, who takes up his LORD's challenge to bargain with him for the lives of those two cities' inhabitants, including his nephew, Lot.

However, notice Abraham's bold humility in addressing God in Genesis 18:27, 28, "Then Abraham spoke up again: 'Now that I have been so bold as to speak to the Lord, though I am nothing but dust and ashes, what if the number of righteous is five less than fifty? Will you destroy the whole city because of five people?'

"'If I find forty-five there,' he said, 'I will not destroy it.'"

I believe that God includes Abraham's humble, yet bold prayer in his Word as a model for our need to be "bolder growin' older" in prayer. On the one hand, we imperfect people are totally unworthy of offering our requests to our perfect Maker.

On the other hand, Jesus' life, death, resurrection, and reentry into heaven pave the prayer way to our heavenly Father.

We are also merely "dust and ashes" and made of Adam stuff, but Jesus raises us to God's throne room as his advisors. Doesn't that thought knock your socks off?

The upshot of Abraham's bold, humble prayer is that angels rescue Lot and his daughters, while God destroys the cities of the plain with fire from heaven.

The sad result of persistent unbelief in the whole Bible

That sad result for Sodom and Gomorrah reminds me of the completely sad fate of all stubborn unbelievers, who will be thrown into the lake of burning sulfur in Revelation 20:10, 15, a symbolic picture of their torment of eternal separation from God in hell.

Therefore, all humans naturally plunge proudly into the pinnacle of pride, only to discover too late that their ready, unrepentant rebellion will bring them God's just judgment, resulting in their tragic exile from him. We need to throw ourselves down before him and plead for his mercy through Jesus and to redouble our efforts to witness to and befriend unbelievers.

So that we don't go astray from our path by thinking that the God of justice is only present in the Old Testament and that he changes into a God of love in the New Testament, we examine Romans 1:18 - 3:20. In that passage, Paul begins his presentation of the good news about God's gift to believers of their right standing before the Judge of the universe. The persistent presence of the parabola of pride in humans is the source of Paul's motivation to share the great news about Jesus (Romans 1:16), "I am not ashamed of the gospel, because it is the power of God that brings salvation to everyone who believes: first to the Jew, then to the Gentiles [non-Jews]."

If God rescues us from our great imperfection by our good actions during our life's journey, the most committed Jews like the Pharisee Paul, before he meets the risen Jesus on the road to Damascus, would also be believers. With that brief meeting, Jesus changes the Christ-persecutor Saul to the Christ-preacher Paul. He transforms the same man miraculously and dramatically.

After someone baptizes Paul, who receives his physical and spiritual sight instead of his twofold blindness, he immediately and boldly preaches Jesus as the only way to get right with God the Father through faith in him, as he says in Romans 1:17. Then, in verses 18-20, Paul describes God's right response to human selfism, "The wrath of God is being revealed from heaven against all the godlessness and wickedness of human beings who suppress the truth by their wickedness, since what may be known about God is plain to them, because God has made it plain to them. For since the creation of the world God's invisible qualities—his eternal power and divine nature—have been clearly seen, being understood by what has been made, so that people are without excuse."

Paul makes some key points here as follows:

(1) Paul eagerly wants to share the good news about the only way to receive the right standing and living that pleases God (verse 16), because all humans have plunged in their parabola of pride to the sinkhole of sinful self-centeredness.

(2) God the Judge's response is right wrath, which includes his just guilty verdict that he pronounces against all humans.

(3) Why? Humans are legally guilty because all human beings have put away God's truth.

(4) God's truth is that he has revealed his divine nature to all humans—that is, his power as the only Creator—through all created things and people.

(5) When we will all stand before God at his Final Judgment, we will have no excuse for rejecting him as the Source of our security, because he has already revealed his power abundantly in his creation. "For although they knew God, they neither glorified him as God nor gave thanks to him, but their thinking became futile and their foolish hearts were darkened" (Romans 1:21). Humans' experience ends in darkened degradation because of our rebellious rejection of our only right Ruler.

Thus, our security in life is only in our Creator-Rescuer, not in our accumulated wealth or our good actions. Paul's point is that we are all under God's just condemnation with his "guilty" verdict and on our way to eternal hell—that is, eternal separation from him because of our self-centered imperfection.

God's final solution to human selfism

However, only the Christian faith, rightly understood, says that God's rescue is fully free and that God gives us his power through Jesus' victory by the Spirit's power to enable us to serve him acceptably.

Therefore, our rightful Creator-Judge completely knows our rebellion in our perilous pursuit of the parabola of pride, justly declares us "guilty," and correctly gives us the death penalty of eternal absence from him as a result of his just wrath—unless he himself, the 3-in-1 God, rescues us.

Without Jesus Christ's death in our place, the potholes on our path toward our final destination become sinkholes.

I pray daily that God will change my selfish pride to submissive peace, for there's a lot of self-centeredness left in my sinful nature during my retirement as Bruce Leiter the Writer. God has led me to pray daily prayers, as I surrender my self-centered desires and my whole life to Jesus.

Bible Discussion Questions:

1. Read Romans 2:1--3:20. In what ways does Paul build his case that the people brought up with God's Word are guilty before our heavenly Judge? How do we know that God has circumcised us inwardly? Explain.
2. How can God use this passage to change how we treat other people? What does Paul mean by the sin of judging others (2:1-11)?
3. How is judging or condemning others different from discerning and avoiding sin? How can we overcome any judging or condemning attitudes that we might have? How are the people described in 2:7 different from the other people's situation in the rest of Romans 1:18--3:20? How can we develop the persistence that Paul describes in 2:7?

* * *

One Step on Our Journey with Jesus: Admit and confess persistently your completely guilty imperfection before God and seek the inner peace that reflects Jesus' gift of outer peace with our Judge.

* * *

I have used a lot of space describing our sinful self-centeredness in order to put in perspective the new creation into which God has transformed us. Our joyful thankfulness and deep love result from our realization that our rescue from the dark depths of depravity is 100 percent to God's credit.

Thus, on our tremendous trip toward eternity, God moves us ...

1. Toward our new God-centeredness:

Becoming more like Jesus

The following quotes show God's grace to deal with pain in old age:

Charles Kingsley: "Pain is no evil, unless it conquers us."

Charles Spurgeon: "I am certain that I never did grow in grace one-half as much anywhere as I have on a bed of pain."

Elizabeth Elliott: "In my own life, I think I can honestly say that out of the deepest pain has come the strongest conviction of the presence of God and the love of God."

Jerry Bridges: "God never allows pain without a purpose in the lives of his children. He never allows Satan, nor circumstances, nor any ill-intending person to afflict us unless he uses that affliction for our good. God never wastes pain. He always causes it to work together for our ultimate good, the good of conforming us more to the likeness of his Son."

How can we become God-centered instead of self-centered in middle and old age like these four people? The Bible's answer is that though the Creator creates the human race in the humble role of creatures under him, he gives us his commission to rule the rest of creation as God's servants who are like him: "Then God said, 'Let us make human beings in our image, in our likeness, so that they may rule over the fish in the sea and the birds in the sky, over the livestock and all the wild animals, and over all the creatures that move along the ground" (Genesis 1:26). Moses here describes the divine Ruler's delegation to humans of authority over the animal creation.

Similarly, Eve's function is to be Adam's assistant in taking care of Eden. Furthermore, Abraham's descendants through Isaac and Jacob are to be God's assistants in taking care of their inheritance, the Promised Land. The Canaanites, like Adam and Eve, rebelliously forfeit their roles in ruling Canaan and their very lives, though God gives them 440 years to repent (Genesis 15:13-16), while Israel is in Egyptian slavery and as God's people wander in the Sinai wasteland.

Likewise, in the New Testament, Jesus says that God gives the earth to the "meek" as his gift of covenant inheritance, according to Jesus' Sermon on the Mount: "Blessed are the meek, for they will inherit the earth" (Matthew 5:5).

At any rate, Psalm 8 describes humans' original, high position in God's creation as a reason for giving praise to the Creator: "You have made them a little lower than the heavenly beings and crowned them with glory and honor.... LORD, our Lord, how majestic is your name in all the earth" (verses 5, 9). Look here at the high position we humans have before our precipitous plunge into rebellious ruin. The free gift of our high place ruling all creation under God's rule, however, isn't good enough for our ancestors.

God's covenant with all believers

The turning point of God the Creator-Judge's relationship with the human race comes when God makes his covenant-relationship with Abram. God seeks personal and community relationships with humans by suddenly appearing to Abram in Genesis 12. Instead of directly dealing with the nations, God renews his relationship with Abram to share his amazing blessings and to call him to obedience. God promises to make childless, seventy-five-year-old Abram "into a great nation," give him abundant blessings, amplify his name, make him a blessing to the nations, and protect him (verses 2,3).

That relationship with individuals and the whole community is called God's covenant, a combination of both his promised blessings and human responsibilities. God also makes that same covenant in a new form with all true believers, who have a personal trust in the 3-in-1 God, since he calls Abram and them into a trust relationship with him (Romans 4; Galatians 3; 2 Corinthians 3:6).

Later, God renews his covenant with Abram by giving him a vision in Genesis 15, when the LORD repeats his promises. However,

Abram questions God's promises of blessings, since he remains childless, until God repeats his promises that old-man Abram's descendants will be as numerous as the stars. Then comes the key description that the New Testament quotes often as the connection between God and believers, "Abram believed the LORD, and he credited it to him as righteousness" (verse 6).

Abram and all believers on their walk with God believe the "unbelievable" by trusting in the invisible God of the impossible. In response to his free gift of trust, God declares that all believers are right with him. That is, he justifies them by anticipating Jesus' Second Coming and looking back on the first coming of the divine-human Descendent of Abram.

Twenty-four years after God first comes to Abram (now renamed Abraham), when childless Abraham is ninety-nine years old, the LORD comes back to him to renew his promises; call him to obedience; and command him to undergo the sign of the covenant—circumcision—which he later replaces with baptism (Colossians 2:12, 13). God restores the covenant relationship by showing his personal love fulfilled in Jesus, the God-man.

The truth of God's covenant is the key to our race on the path through old age and death to Jesus' final victory.

Personal covenant experiences

In my life, God welcomed me into his believing family when I was christened as a Methodist infant and again when I was immersed with water baptism at twelve years old while attending a community church. In those churches and with my believing mother, I was "under" the covenant (receiving God's blessings through them). However, God transformed my life to be "in" his covenant when he gave me faith while attending a Baptist church when I was sixteen years old. For the last fifty-four years, he has continued to change me "in" Jesus, even though I still have a lot of progress to make.

Moreover, the psalms are personal expressions of that same covenant love-relationship. Psalms 6, 22, 39, and 88 are genuine, honest prayers expressing feelings of desperation and depression with open weeping. The psalmist in a personal, covenant commitment calls on the LORD of the covenant to rescue him and thus fulfill his protective promises.

In Psalm 23, David expresses that same covenant relationship as the shepherd-ruler of God's sheep, Israel, as he professes his personal, covenant-love relationship with his divine Shepherd.

In addition, remember that Jesus directly identifies himself, in John chapter ten, with that same divine Shepherd as well as the great "I AM" who appeared to Moses in the unburnable burning bush. Jesus proclaims, "I am the good shepherd ... [who] lays down his life for the sheep.... I am the good shepherd; I know my sheep and my sheep know me" (John 10:11, 14). His words are a description of the new-covenant relationship of self-sacrificial—not self-centered—love between believers and the 3-in-1 God through Jesus. That same covenant takes on a new form, the new covenant or testament, through Jesus' life, death, and resurrection.

Thus, God's initiated relationship with all believers as "children" of Abraham (Galatians 3:29) shows up as his unconditional love. One of the results in believers' lives is praise for God's fulfillment of his promises. For example, Psalm 34 expresses David's praise for God's deliverance, possibly from sickness, that he requests in Psalms 38 and 39.

Furthermore, the psalmists in Psalms 24 and 66 express their joyful gratitude for God's covenant showing of himself to his people and for his covenant answers to prayer, respectively. Also, in Psalm 50, God reveals his covenant faithfulness that accuses his people of only external covenant worship. He calls them to an inner faith commitment shown by thank offerings emphasizing genuine thanksgiving (verse 23).

Therefore, in old age, our thankfulness for Jesus' death and resurrection to rescue us must be sincere generosity focused on God, not ourselves.

The old versus new covenant in our old age

Even though some people have contrasted the Old Testament's external religion with the New Testament's inner religion, we see here that both parts of the Bible emphasize the inner and outer aspects of God's covenant relationship with his people. Of course, the Old Testament centers its attention mostly on the old-covenant nation of Israel, whereas the New Testament centers its focus on an international church in a new-covenant relationship of love with God.

How can we face the fact that we will grow old and die in our so-called "golden years"? We can endure the old age experience and can face death if we accept and live the biblical fact that Jesus' deliverance as our inheritance is like a huge diamond with many facets or angles with much greater value than the largest diamond on earth.

In other words, we must accept his free, costly rescue as our present and future inheritance. Therefore, let's explore the many fabulous facets of his free gift as we travel the path toward our final future in him.

Before he concocts creation, God lovingly chooses his own people as a nation and as a church. He also selects individual believers from among his people in both eras (Romans 8:28-30; Ephesians 1:3-14). In addition, he allows humans' total rebellion as part of his permissive plan for them, even though they have all decided passively or actively to run their own lives. The result is that they are conceived and born slaves to selfishness and Satan, in addition to being dead and deaf to the deity (Ephesians 2:1-3).

Therefore, it is certainly true that we cannot arrive at our final victory by our own efforts to be good, unlike the other religions' teachings. We certainly can't make ourselves alive and able to hear him.

On our sometimes rough road toward our free, final future, we investigate the truth that the 3-in-1 God himself perfectly provides his divine deliverance of believers through Jesus' first coming. The reason is that we cannot possibly rescue ourselves.

God's amazing plan for our restoration

We have arrived at a particularly scenic panorama on our tourist trip to our fabulous future. God's plan to rescue his believers from the fear of the ravages of old age and death is the heavenly Father's well-known plan to send his unique Son as follows: "For God so loved the world that he gave his one and only Son, that whoever believes in him shall not perish but have eternal life" (John 3:16).

God's less-familiar promise and warning in verses 17 and 18 follow, "For God did not send his Son into the world to condemn the world, but to save the world through him. Whoever believes in him is not condemned, but whoever does not believe stands condemned already because they have not believed in the name of God's one and only Son."

It is not God's fault that he as the just Judge condemns people for their unbelief. They have willfully or passively gone astray from his will. Humans certainly cannot earn their way into his acceptance, because they are born diseased, dead, deaf, and darkened by the devil. They are on the slippery slope of sinful selfism, for which they have no one to blame but themselves.

However, the amazing view is that God himself has provided the free solution that makes his people perfect in our Judge's sight and that enables us to overcome our fears of old age and death.

God's free gift as a many-faceted diamond is an amazing inheritance that we will investigate at length.

God's free miracle of the new birth

As we continue our journey toward our final victory, we can find God's strength in old age to face death by examining the first free facet of God's gift of the new birth described in Jesus' words at the beginning of John chapter three. That passage describes Nicodemus' visit to Jesus. This prim and proper Pharisee flatters Jesus as a "teacher who has come from God" (verse 2b). However, Jesus immediately cuts through the fog of Pharisaical flattery by describing to Nicodemus the heart of his matter, "Very truly I tell you, no one can see the kingdom of God without being born again [or "from above"]" (verse 3).

Naturally, Nicodemus misunderstands Jesus' comment as physical birth. Jesus corrects his misunderstanding by saying that the key to entering God's kingdom is to be "born of water and the Spirit" (verse 5). What Jesus means by being born of water is disputable, but it may refer to physical birth. However, his reference to being born of the Spirit clearly refers to the Holy Spirit's change in a person's life that brings about a personal trust in the God-man, Jesus, as our only Pathway to the Father. Knowing Jesus puts us on the right Road to the Ruler.

The word "Spirit" in John chapter three also refers to the Hebrew and Greek words translated "wind" throughout the Bible. Jesus' metaphor in verse 8 compares the Holy Spirit with wind in order to point out his unpredictable, miraculous transformation of unbelievers changed into believers who love and trust in Jesus.

As we believers pause on our lifelong journey to marvel at God's miraculous gift of the new birth, we notice that the Old Testament background points to the real inner meaning of the outward ceremonies of circumcision and baptism. In Deuteronomy 30:1-5, God inspires Moses to prophesy that the people will return from the exile that God will impose in their future because of their predictable wandering into idolatrous selfism. Then, in verse six, he prophesies that the "LORD your God will circumcise your hearts and the hearts of your descendents, so that you may love him with all your heart and with all your soul, and live."

Similarly, Jesus says in John chapter three to Nicodemus that even he, a strict law-abider, had to be born again or "from above".

I praise God that he rescued me by "talking" me into believing in Jesus' resurrection, largely with my reasoning, when I was sixteen years old, and he's still working with my mind. However, though my will was changed somewhat, he shaped it more by permitting our second boy's death. He changed my rebellion that led me into teaching and sales to submission that he used to make me a pastor.

Bible Discussion Questions:

1. How do you feel about the fact that you will appear before God to be judged "guilty" or "not guilty"? What assurance do you have that he will pronounce you "not guilty"? Why?
2. Read John 3:1-18. What exactly did God do to rescue you from slavery to sin and Satan, according to all of these verses? How do you feel about the miracle of the new birth that all believers have received (verses 3-8)? Explain.
3. Where did Jesus come from (John 3:13)? Why did he come (verses 14-17)? What basic, different destinations do believers and unbelievers have in their future (verse 18)? How do we know whether we are believers or unbelievers? Explain.

* * *

One Step on Our Journey with Jesus: Admit and accept the fact that you cannot in any way earn God's acceptance and love on your own, because you are incapable of pleasing God in your own power. Confess daily your inability to please him in your own strength, and ask him for his power through Jesus' victory by the Spirit's presence to live for him.

***

Our baptism with the Holy Spirit and fire

More comfort concerning believers' new birth comes from John the Baptist, who prophesies Jesus' first coming, "I baptize you with water for repentance. But after me comes one who is more powerful than I, whose sandals I am not worthy to carry. He will baptize you with the Holy Spirit and fire" (Matthew 3:11). John refers to the same change described in all of these passages. The Holy Spirit baptizes believers with himself and with God's refining fire when we first trust in Jesus as the Corridor to our heavenly Father, our Creator.

Paul summarizes the meaning of the new birth in Romans 7:6, "But now, by dying to what once bound us, we have been released from the law so that we serve in the new way of the Spirit, and not in the old way of the written code." Believers never have a relationship with rules, regulations, as the people of other religions and the cults do. Instead, believers' personal, covenant relationship with their one, only true God is the only source of the new life that lasts beyond death.

Then, Paul describes in Romans 6:7-23 his own personal experience of the wrestling match within true believers between the old and new natures throughout the rest of our lives, until he finally exclaims, "What a wretched man I am! Who shall rescue me from this body of death? Thanks be to God, who delivers me through Jesus Christ our Lord!" (verses 24,25).

Importantly, a key Bible passage in our attempt to understand the nature of our new-birth facet is Ephesians 2:1-10. People approach God from two extremes. On the one hand, the other world belief-systems as well as the cults that have come out of Christianity claim that we can please God on his scales of goodness by doing more good than bad works. On the other hand, a number of people believe that they can go on sinning and merely ask for and receive forgiveness without changing at all. In both extreme belief-systems, people think that only human effort or sorrow without changes in their personalities can get God's approval.

However, God inspires Paul to take a different approach. In Ephesians 2:1-3, he claims that we are spiritually stillborn like a fake diamond. We are all born dead to God and alienated from him. He declares, "You were dead in your transgressions and sins" (verse 1), as every one of us follow Satan's and our own selfish ways beginning at our conception and birth. "Like the rest, we were by nature deserving of wrath [echoing Romans 1:18-20]. But because of his great love for us, God, who is rich in mercy, made us alive with Christ, even when we were dead in transgressions—it is by grace you have been saved" (Ephesians 2:3b-5).

An amazing experience

When I returned to one of my churches for their seventy-fifth anniversary, a woman in her thirties related her experience as a middle-schooler when I was her pastor. One Sunday morning when I preached on Ephesians two, I said, "We are all born dead." This girl, who had never previously listened to any preacher's messages, suddenly wondered what I meant. I went on to say that we are spiritually stillborn because at birth we cannot respond to God through faith in Jesus. This woman has been eagerly listening to messages and serving him in his church ever since God's awakening that Sunday morning. I was thankful that God gave her his miracle during my message.

Paul's and John's inspired descriptions of the new birth

Thus, Paul's inspired answer to all human, self-help groups that are insecure about old age and death is that God gives his rescue solely with his free, unconditional, undeserved acceptance—his grace—not at all by human effort or emotion, but only because of Jesus' life, death, and resurrection.

As a result, such a set of beliefs cannot have come from human thought. Christian ideas are far from human inventions. They definitely come from God.

What happens when God makes us alive through his free gift of the new birth? "And God raised us up with Christ and seated us with him in the heavenly realms in Christ Jesus" (Ephesians 2:6) with a future, final fulfillment. If, in principle, we are already in heaven with Jesus, how can we live anymore in the old way of selfishness and be petrified by the prospect of growing old and dying?

Paul goes on to point out that God's rescue comes to us as his free gift by grace through faith—a personal trust in the 3-in-1 God—not by self-help (verses 8 and 9).

Then, Paul's inspired balance avoids some people's charge that such a free gift produces unrestrained sin by adding tellingly, "For we are God's handiwork, created in Christ Jesus to do good works, which God prepared in advance for us to do" (verse 10). The Greek word translated "handiwork" refers to an artistic work like a painting or a sculpture. The Christian life is like God's painting in progress that he will complete when he resurrects our bodies. Just as an artist visualizes the final product of his painting before he slaps paint on his canvas, God as the divine Painter is gradually painting our lives to be more and more like him, just as God originally made Adam. God's progress begins with our Spirit-baptism that causes the new birth.

The apostle John sheds further light on the new-birth change in 1 John 2:8, 9: "Yet I am writing you a new command; its truth is in him and in you, because the darkness is passing and the true light is already shining. Those who claim to be in the light but hate a fellow believer are still in the darkness." God shows his unconditional love through Jesus' sacrificial death entirely for believers' benefit, totally unworthy though we are. That love transforms believers gradually to love unlovable people, just as we are God's unlovable objects of his love as well.

Therefore, if we are trying to rescue ourselves through our imperfect actions while traveling a false life path with the fake diamond of our own goodness, we *should* be insecure about old age and death, because we are really on the wrong road. However, God provides his solution for our dead condition. All we need to do is accept his solution to replace our own efforts with faith in Jesus Christ's work for us.

I can understand people's desires to escape or deny old age and death, because I have a tendency toward escapism. I pray daily that God will replace that old-nature quality with endurance.

Bible Discussion Questions:

1. Read Ephesians 2:1-10. In what sense do we arrive in this world spiritually stillborn? Why do some people believe that babies are innocent? What evidence is there that they are really dead in their sins? Explain by giving examples.
2. How does God make believers spiritually alive? Give a personal example of your life or someone else's experience.
3. Define in your own words God's grace and the meaning of faith (verses 8, 9). What are the results in our lives of God's free deliverance (verse 10)? How do you know that he has rescued you? Explain.

* * *

One Step on Our Journey with Jesus: If you haven't already accepted Jesus Christ's life, death, and resurrection as God's only way for you to be rescued, ask him for his free gift of the new birth. If you have, praise him daily for his amazing gift of the new birth by his grace (free acceptance). "Be bolder growin' older" in prayer for endurance in life's struggles as you approach and endure old age.

* * *

On our journey with Jesus toward our final bliss,

he wants us to move ...

Chapter Two: *From* Old Feelings of Worthlessness *to* New Feelings of Worth:

2. <u>From old feelings of worthlessness:</u>

The second temptation of old age in addition to selfishness, according to Keith Drury's research, is that older folks often feel worthless because they can no longer contribute to society.

Why do older people, even Christians, feel useless? Often, even Christians have accepted our society's emphasis on being productive in a paying job as the source of our usefulness. When we can no longer productively contribute to society, we feel useless. This temptation to sin is especially evident among those among us with a strong work ethic.

Why do we lean on productive work for our self-esteem? It seems to me that productivity can be an idol in our lives stemming from the idea of pragmatism, a philosophy teaching that what works is good.

When we no longer work, we might get depressed or replace work with another idol like pleasure as our escape. So goes our modern society's idolatry.

Instead, as Christians, let's rise above our culture's dependence on work or pleasure to make us feel good about ourselves. If we have neither work nor pleasure to keep us going, we can still have God, who is always with us.

Our culture's negative influence

Society may consider older people worthless, but why should culture influence us older Christians to evaluate our lives that way?

Furthermore, if we look at the staggering evidence in the Bible about our selfish sinfulness, we might be tempted to consider ourselves worthless as well because of our feelings of guilt about our past sins.

We also have more time to reflect on the past during our older years. As a result, we can get mired down in our dirty past actions.

Moreover, we can carry with us negative thoughts and grudges against people who have acted unlovingly toward us. We can also transfer negative thoughts about others to ourselves.

Therefore, Keith Drury comments, "An old person is sometimes treated as dead weight to society…. Retired folk find that they have more time on their hands than ever, but they sometimes have less to do. One said to me, 'I get up earlier but have no place to go' and another, 'I'm busier than ever doing less than ever.'" He goes on to observe that older people and their families often compare their less active lives to the people he calls the "active aged," a comparison that is unfair.

For example, the result is that the less active aged struggling with health issues feel worthless if they haven't been able to reach the bottom of the Grand Canyon like some more healthy old folks have been able to do. We saw that Colossal Canyon last year, and the only way that I would ever reach its bottom is by accidentally falling there. Thankfully, God protected me from that result.

However, though the Bible pulls no punches about our sinful depravity, it helps us overcome our sinfulness through Jesus Christ.

When I retired the first time from the ministry because of the vicious disease of depression, I grieved for a whole year over my loss of preaching and teaching as a pastor. The trouble was that my ego and worth were tied to those activities and my career. God taught me through that grief process to separate preaching from my ego so that being a preacher became only one of my many roles of friend, preacher, teacher, father, husband, and grandfather. By God's leading, I no longer identified those roles with me, but they became activities that I did. Then God healed me and restored my calling. In my remaining four churches, when people criticized my messages or other actions, they were no longer challenging my ego but my actions. Thus, God liberated me from defensiveness and from the idolatry of work.

On our journey with Jesus, God wants to move us from old feelings of worthlessness …

2. **To new feelings of worth:**

How can God help us overcome feelings of worthlessness?

Let's look at Bible passages that teach our worth before God. We begin in Genesis. In chapter 1:27, an inspired Moses writes, "God created man in his own image, in the image of God he created him; male and female he created them." If God makes us to be like him in some ways, we definitely have value to him, even after we fall into sin with Adam and Eve. Why else would God love the world so much as to send his unique Son, Jesus, to die on the Roman torture instrument in order to give us life to replace our spiritual death? As a result, all humans have worth in his sight because he creates them.

In addition, after Adam and Eve rebel against God through their disobedience, God doesn't write them off by killing them but comes to Eden to seek them out. After they hide from him, "The LORD God called out to the man, 'Where are you?'" (Genesis 3:9). He then calls them to their responsibility for their actions without excusing them. Thus, God affirms their worth as he seeks their confession and transformation. Typically, they justify themselves by blaming God and each other.

Similarly, God confronts Cain's sin before he commits murder (Genesis 4:6,7). Afterward, God points out Cain's transgression but mercifully puts his mark on Cain rather than summarily executing him on the spot because of his murder (4:10-12).

Similarly, the same pattern goes throughout the Bible. At the time of Noah, God gives humanity 120 years to turn back to him while Noah builds a dry-docked ship to prepare for the flood. Furthermore, God allows the Israelites to be slaves in Egypt partly to give the pagan people of Canaan 400 years to trust in him rather than their false gods (see Genesis 15:13-16). God also uses Moses' prayers to postpone his punishment for the Israelites' unbelief for forty years of desert wandering while that generation dies out, thus postponing God's judgment on the Canaanites another forty years. Finally, Jesus prays on the cross for the Father to forgive his crucifiers in order to give them time to have faith in him after his resurrection.

These examples all point to God's estimation of our worth as his creations. However, a day will come for humanity to be accountable to God at Jesus' Final Judgment when he returns.

In addition to these examples, God favors humanity greatly with the events of Jesus' conception and birth as the God-baby, his perfect life as the God-man resisting all temptations, his agonizingly-painful suffering and death to take away our guilt, and his resurrection to give us new and growing life.

However, as with many other issues, God's ways are not our culture's ways. We have worth in his sight even while we sit days and weeks on end in a nursing home. Just as the helpless baby in the womb has God's estimate of worth, so the cripple in a nursing facility has worth, more so if that person is a Christian. I have told people in such places that if they have their minds, they can be God's worthwhile prayer-warriors for people that they know, their churches, and their nation. They have God's prayer-career.

God can even use people with dementia to give other people opportunities to show their love by visiting them.

The comfort of the Book of Job

The Book of Job should be a source of great comfort to us as we anticipate the losses of old age and death on our unstoppable trip toward those events. God allows Satan to inflict huge suffering on believing Job (chapters one and two) as the devil attempts to break his faith in God, which remains in spite of severe losses (Job 2:10). However, in chapter three, Job openly expresses his grief by lamenting the day of his birth, indirectly questioning God's plan for his birth and life. His "friends" directly and indirectly reflect the religious thinking of their day by condemning Job for some great sin that he must have done, thus resulting in his great tragedies.

Job also has the same ideas when he protests that he has been faithfully committed to God. Thus, he questions why God allows his deep, difficult suffering, since he has committed no huge offenses against God. In chapters 38-41, God confronts Job with his informed questions by asking him if he creates the creatures in the world, thus putting Job in his place as the creature, not the Creator. Job's humble repentance is the result (42:1-6). Then, God expresses his anger at

Job's so-called friends, "I am angry with you [Eliphaz] and your two friends, because you have not spoken of me what is right, as my servant Job has" (42:7b).

Why does God commend Job for his words but not his "friends"? I believe that the true God of the Bible values open, genuine honesty in our prayer life like Job's prayers similar to the Psalms.

On the other hand, the three men condemn Job with their judgmentalism. They jump to negative conclusions about Job's guilt when he is blameless of great transgressions.

Thus, God wants us to unload our anger and anxiety on him in prayer the way Job did, rather than unloading them on other people, the way the "friends" did to Job with their "superior" judgmentalism and condemnation. As a result, God uses Job as the other men's priest standing in the gap between God and them to prevent his severe punishment (42:8, 9).

Thus, if you are a living human being, you have worth in your Creator's estimate. If you are a true believer in him, you have so much amazing worth that he listens to your prayers in his heavenly throne room 24/7. Thus, you have twenty-four hour access to him as his committed Christian, even if you are no longer a productive member of our society. Your productivity is prayer. Our thought life should, therefore, be filled with prayer and praise all day long (see 1 Thessalonians 5:16-18).

Paul's calls to be strong in Jesus' power

Furthermore, consider Ephesians 6:10-20. In that passage, God calls us to be his soldiers in his army against Satan's army, from which we do not retire because of age. At the time that Paul writes those words guided by God, he experiences house arrest in Rome, awaiting trial before notoriously unpredictable Emperor Nero. He is chained to a Roman soldier much of the time. As a result, he compares our warlike armor to the protective dress of the Roman infantryman. He begins this section with the two commands for us "to be strong in the Lord and in his mighty power" and to "put on the whole armor of God ..." (verses 10, 11).

Why? Paul doesn't say that he is fighting against Nero or the Roman soldiers. Similarly, our enemies are not human because God's Word makes it clear through Paul that our "struggle is not against flesh and blood but ... against the spiritual forces of evil in the heavenly realms" (verse 12). Thus, Paul calls us to put on God's protection against the devil and demons.

A lot of people dismiss the idea that the creation is filled with evil spiritual angels who try to overcome us. However, the Bible is clear that the devil and demons exist as our opposition if we are Christians. They are our enemies, not people. The Book of Job reveals the same truth.

Notice the parts of our Provider's protection: the belt of truth, breastplate of righteousness, sandals of the gospel of peace, shield of faith, helmet of salvation, and sword of the Word of God. Thus, God calls us to exercise our faith by reading the Bible and trusting in him through prayer to protect us, our loved ones, and our churches against the devil's temptations as we approach and enter old age.

We can also find his gift of hopeful courage as we face death.

Notice also Paul's final command in Ephesians 6:18, "And pray in the Spirit on all occasions with all kinds of prayers. With this in mind, be alert and always keep on praying for all the saints." For Paul, prayer is like the straps that hold the Roman's armor together.

Some people interpret praying in the Spirit as some special kind of prayer, but it's clear in this passage that it means all prayers guided by the Holy Spirit. Similar meaning is found in Romans 8:26, 27, where Paul writes that the Spirit overcomes our weaknesses in prayer by praying for and with us. Thus, God calls us to "be bolder growin' older," primarily through courageous prayer. We older folks have more time for prayer and should pray more.

Where we can gain strength in old age

James writes in 4:7, "Submit yourselves, then, to God. Resist the devil, and he will flee from you." Therefore, God definitely wants us to "be bolder growin' older" in prayerfully resisting evil influences in our lives and other people's lives through Jesus' triumph. These two commands have a promise that God will make the devil and the demons flee from us as believers. We need to follow his command and prayerfully claim his promise as we experience the warfare between God and his evil opposition.

Prayerless people experience defeat.

How much more worth can we have as God's empowered soldiers praying and living in his victory through Jesus by the Holy Spirit? Of course, Jesus gives us his strength because we cannot battle the devil's temptations and schemes with our own power. Ask your Father for his strength daily through Jesus by way of the Spirit.

In God's eyes, we are unworthy of his love but far from worthless as his creatures and as Christians.

While I was growing up in a dysfunctional family, my parents favored my brothers, not me. I tried to please them and my teachers in school but never felt their love. Jesus overcame that loneliness by coming into my life when I was sixteen years old. He showed me his unconditional love and free acceptance (grace) by giving me faith in him.

Bible Discussion Questions:

1. In your own words, explain how much value you are to God. How and why does the Book of Job encourage you? Explain.
2. How does Ephesians 6:10-20 give you hope in overcoming the temptations of old age? Why?
3. How can we incorporate James 4:17 into our lives? Explain.
4. Specifically, how has this section helped your Christian life? Why?

* * *

One Step on Our Journey with Jesus: Resolve to give your thought-life to God to pray to God against the devil and for God's victory in your life and in the lives of people you know. Also, give your thoughts to praising the 3-in-1 God's greatness.

* * *

As we travel our tourist trip toward God's final kingdom, he wants us to plod his path ...

Chapter Three: *From* old selfish use of money *to* new generosity

3. From old, selfish use of money

Observations about wealth

Keith Drury writes, "Not all older people have more money than they need, but if they do, they will be tempted to cling more tightly to their money.... It is difficult for people of all ages to be generous, but it is especially hard for older people."

One reason for older people's stinginess is fear that their money will run out because of disability. Thus, "at no age is the sin of trusting money so prevalent as among the old" (Keith Drury's Internet article "The Temptations of Old Age," with full permission-- http://www.drurywriting.com/keith/sins.of.old.age.htm).

My experiences with people who have gone through life's school of hard knocks confirms that many of them stash their money away and only reluctantly give it to worthy causes. Others become more generous when God blesses them more.

We need to search our motives for the use or lack of use of our money. Selfishness can be the driving force in clinging to it and also in giving it generously. Self-centered fear of its running out can be our motivation. Also, giving it away because we want to control our family with our wealth and because our giving gives us a positive feeling are both sinful, selfish reasons.

In addition, using our money for our own selfish pleasure is, of course, wrong. One bumper sticker on an RV says, "We're spending our children's inheritance." Of course, hoarding our wealth in order to give our children all of our resources is also selfish motivation. Perhaps, we could also try to get our family's admiration or to make up for our parental failures.

I have seen many family situations in which children squabble over their parents' wealth after they die and stop talking to each other. In one family, the father of three daughters died without a will. One daughter grabbed the cottage at the lake; another, the house in town. The third was left with the father's pasture land. The three women didn't speak to each other for many years.

That incident provokes my suggestion that it's best to spell out in a will exactly how you want to pass on your wealth when you die.

Anyway, money and selfishness often go hand in hand.

The Bible's teachings about money and wealth

Several biblical passages illustrate the pitfalls of stinginess. For example, Jesus tells a parable in Luke 12:13-21 that is introduced with a person in the crowd calling on Jesus to be a judge of a family dispute, "Tell my brother to divide the inheritance with me."

Jesus disavows being the family's judge. Some day he will come to judge all people justly, but he comes the first time to save, not judge, people. Then, he says pointedly, "Watch out! Be on your guard against all kinds of greed; a man's life does not consist in the abundance of his possessions" (Luke 12:15).

He drives home his direct commands with a familiar parable about a rich farmer who has a good crop and decides to tear his barns down and build bigger ones. Then he decides to retire and live a life of leisure. God's responds, "You fool! This very night your life will be demanded from you. Then who will get what you have prepared for yourself?" (verse 20).

Jesus' commentary makes the parable's meaning very clear, "This is how it will be with anyone who stores up things for himself but is not rich toward God." Since the rich man is addicted to money, wealth, and pleasure, his reward is only in this life, not the next.

In the Old Testament, God's principle is that because the Garden of Eden belongs to him and because his human creatures are only its caretakers, he evicts Adam and Eve due to their self-centered rebellion against him.

Similarly, God shares a principle about the land of Canaan that he gives to Israel in Leviticus 25:23 about the return of sold land when the fiftieth jubilee year arrives: "The land must not be sold permanently, because the land is mine and you are but aliens and my tenants."

On the contrary, God's principle is that *he* owns all that we have and that we are mere renters taking care of it for him. The psalmist says under God's inspiration, "The earth is the LORD's and everything in it, the world and all who live in it, for he founded it upon the seas and established it upon the waters" (Psalm 24:1).

You see, the Bible as God's Word turns all human thinking on its head. Therefore, God is definitely its Source, since no humans would have come up with its truths.

The New Testament's teachings about money and possessions

Jesus bluntly teaches in his Sermon on the Mount, "Do not store up for yourselves treasures on earth, where moth and rust destroy, and where thieves break in and steal. But store up for yourselves treasures in heaven, where moth and rust do not destroy, and where thieves do not break in and steal. For where your treasure is, there your heart will be also.... No one can serve two masters. Either he will hate the one and love the other, or he will be devoted to one and despise the other. You cannot serve both God and Money" (Matthew 6:19-21, 24). Our hearts must be set on pleasing our heavenly Father unselfishly and lovingly by using the income with which he has blessed us.

Therefore, since we will lose our treasures on earth when we die, the treasures that we build up in heaven through our loving actions will be his awesome blessings when we enter heaven as believers after death and when Jesus gives us the new creation at his return. Giving generously to good Christian causes builds up our treasure in heaven that we will enjoy forever in God's powerful presence.

My point is that all of the money and things with which God has blessed us belong to him. Let's give all of them back to him to be used with thanksgiving.

A preacher who lived in the early 1900s rightly said to his congregation, "If you can use a luxury to honor God and if buying it will not decrease your generous giving, then you can go ahead and buy it."

One more New Testament passage clearly points out the dangers of focusing our lives on our money and possessions, I Timothy 6:9, 10, 17, "People who want to get rich fall into temptation and a trap and into many foolish and harmful desires that plunge men into ruin and destruction. For the love of money is a root of all kinds of evil. Some people, eager for money, have wandered from the faith and pierced themselves with many griefs.... Command those who are rich in this present world not to be arrogant nor to put their hope in wealth, which is so uncertain, but to put their hope in God, who richly provides us with everything for our enjoyment."

Notice that it's not whether we have a lot of money and material things, but it's our focus that matters to God. He blesses us with things with which we can rejoice in him as the Creator of his world.

God has blessed me with a 50" HD TV with surround-sound speakers and a computer with a 23" LED monitor and a good printer in my "man-cave" basement room. Some people would suspect that I am caught up in materialism and excess, but God has guided me to give all of my electronics to God. He has enabled me to choose TV sports, "justice dramas," and other programs with which I praise him as the just Creator.

I'm also thankful that he has given me tools with which I can write and promote books that honor him. He gave me those insights, all to his praise!

Keith Drury comments, "The aged look around and see other old people who have been abandoned to fend for themselves and they get fearful they will be left with nothing. It is difficult for people of all ages to be generous, but it is especially hard for older people…. The aged are tempted to trust in Mammon [money] to save them…. Money may bring security, but it will not bring joy."

Thus, as we travel his trip, God wants us to move from selfish use of money …

3. **To new generosity**

God's generosity guidelines

When we got married, we felt God's leading to give at least a tenth of our income to God's church and legitimate causes spreading his Word. We also felt the desire to send our children to Christian schools that taught in agreement with God's biblical principles. As a result, God blessed us by providing for our family's needs and more. God receives our praise for his blessing on the desires that he prompted in us.

How, then, can we develop a new generosity in the use of our income? The apostle Paul writes about that subject in 2 Corinthians 8 and 9 without using the word "money."

In one of my churches I discovered that when I used the word "money," it caused a negative reaction that blocked communication. As a result, I used other words like "income" or "wealth" that didn't have the same reaction.

Perhaps, Paul's method is similar. At any rate, he encourages the church in Corinth to give generously to help the Jerusalem Christians, who experience a famine. In looking at these chapters, we can discover God's seven inspired motivations for generosity as follows:

(1) Paul first points to northern Greece, Macedonian churches' great generosity even in their poverty, "Now, brothers, we want you to know about the grace that God has given the Macedonian churches. Out of the most severe trial, their overflowing joy and extreme poverty welled up in rich generosity" (1 Corinthians 8:1, 2).

Notice that God's grace enables us to give generously. What is that grace? God accepts us freely by grace only because of Jesus' life and death as our Substitute. That free acceptance earned by Jesus comes into our lives as believers, resulting in our free acceptance of others because we love Jesus.

The result must be our generosity in response to God's free rescue. Later, at the end of verse six, Paul uses the term "act of grace" for the Corinthians' potential gift.

Also, our response to God's amazing grace is "overflowing joy." How can we not be joyful because of Jesus' free life, death, and resurrection accomplished for us who are completely undeserving? The result must be free, joyful generosity in our giving.

After all, Paul wrote that "God loves a cheerful giver" in chapter 9:7 by describing a motive that points to the Greek word for cheerfulness, the English word *hilarity*. Again, free generosity is the opposite of forced reluctance or grudging giving, according to that same verse.

(2) Then, in 8:5, Paul describes another basis for generosity. The Macedonians "gave themselves first to the Lord and then to us in keeping with God's will." Thus, because of God's grace and will, we need to surrender ourselves and our wealth to God for others' benefit.

(3) Paul goes on to describe true giving as being motivated by complete earnestness and love (8:8), "For you know the grace of our Lord Jesus Christ, that though he was rich, yet for your sakes, he became poor, so that you through his poverty might become rich"

(verse nine). Therefore, the ultimate motive for our giving is Jesus' descent from the glorious, high status of heaven as God to become a comparatively very poor God-man so that he makes us rich. After all, he says, "Blessed are the meek, for they will inherit the earth."

Even now, we are rich in God's blessings. Those riches must motivate us to give to those in need for their good in loving response to Jesus' self-sacrifice for us.

(4) Another of God's purposes is that he wants equality among his people (8:13-15). Paul urges the Corinthians to give "hilariously" in order to supply the needs of the Jerusalem Christians. Then, at some point, God may supply the Corinthians' needs. However, our motive must not be to give in order to get, a possible interpretation of the phrase "paying it forward." We must never give in order to pay God or people off.

(5) Paul says that he will administer the gift "in order to honor the Lord himself and to show our eagerness to help" (8:19). Here, we see the vertical and horizontal dimensions of giving. We must give generously and eagerly to honor God and to help others.

(6) Another biblical principle for our giving is the sowing and reaping comparison. "Remember this: Whoever sows sparingly will also reap sparingly, and whoever sows generously will also reap generously. Each man should give what he has decided in his heart to give, not reluctantly or under compulsion, for God

loves a cheerful giver. And God is able to make all grace abound to you, so that in all things in all times, having all that you need, you will abound in every good work.... Now he who supplies seed to the sower and bread for food will also supply and increase your store of seed and will enlarge the harvest of your righteousness" (verses 8, 10). Notice that our sowing of our money will result in a harvest of our righteousness. However, our sowing with giving in no way earns the harvest. The "seeds," our sowing, and the result all are God's gifts of grace.

Of course, God promises to provide for our needs and to increase our spiritual commitment to him and to those in need, but he does not promise to make us materially rich. Thus, our giving goal must not be to get more stuff or wealth that we can hoard. In other words, God wants our giving to be God- and other-centered, not self-centered.

(7) Paul's seventh point about giving is that it will result in overflowing thankfulness in the recipients' lives (2 Corinthians 9:12-15). He then ends this section appropriately, "Thanks be to God for his indescribable gift!" (verse 16). God the Father gave us Jesus. We should therefore show our loving response by giving generously.

Our generous giving's quantity

Now that we have seen the quality of our giving, we consider its quantity. The prophet Malachi preaches to the returned exiles, whom God accuses of robbing him, "But you ask, 'How do we rob you?' 'In tithes and offerings. You are under a curse—the whole nation of you—because you are robbing me. Bring the whole tithe into the storehouse, that there may be food in my house. Test me in this,' says the LORD Almighty, 'and see if I will not throw open the floodgates of heaven and pour out so much blessing that you will not have room enough for it....Then all the nations will call you blessed, for yours will be a delightful land,' says the LORD Almighty" (Malachi 3:8b-10, 12).

Notice that God wants us to give more than a tenth (tithe) of our income to his church and spiritual causes ("tithes *and* offerings"). One result is that he will bless us abundantly with spiritual and material provisions. Another is that the nations will respond with thanks to the true God.

One note is necessary. When fund-raisers call me for donations, I always ask them what percentage of my gift will actually get to the people for whom it is intended. They have to answer truthfully by law. If less than 80 percent goes to the people for whom it is intended, too much is going to the fund-raiser.

When one of those called the other day, he quickly said 80 percent before I was able to finish my question, but he meant that that amount went to the fund-raiser. Most of them say that only 15 percent to 20 percent actually goes to the veterans, police, or other causes. However, my response to the quick caller was that I only give to spread the gospel, and he hung up on me!

On the other hand, if you consider giving to a certain cause, I suggest that you ask for a recently-audited financial statement to see where your gift actually goes and a list of their beliefs (if they claim to be Christian) before you give. Also, commit your giving to prayer, and God will lead you.

In addition, in Genesis 14, Abram rescues his nephew Lot, who has become a prisoner of war, from his captors' clutches. Afterwards, "Melchizedek king of [Jerusalem] brought out bread and wine. He was priest of God Most High, and he blessed Abram.... Then Abram gave him a tenth of everything [the war plunder]" (verses 18 and 19). Thus, Abram modeled generous giving for all of his spiritual and physical children. We believers are his "children" by faith (see Galatians 3:29 and Romans 4).

Furthermore, so that we don't think that tithing is only an Old Testament command, I point you to the time a Pharisee invites Jesus to a meal (Luke 11:37). The Pharisees are surprised that Jesus fails to do the usual ceremonial washing before eating. In response, Jesus states six indictments of their external religion.

The second criticism follows: "Woe to you Pharisees, because you give God a tenth of your mint, rue, and all other kinds of garden herbs, but you neglect justice and the love of God. You should have practiced the latter without leaving the former undone" (Luke 11:42). Thus, Jesus confirms his approval of giving at least a tenth of our income and showing our love to God by our generosity.

Now, if our needs, not our wants, take up more than 90 percent of our income, we need to pray to our God, who understands. We also need to reign in our spending on our wants so that we can tithe the first part of our income as our firstfruits to the Lord (see Exodus 23:16).

When I first became a Christian, I shared the biblical principle of tithing with family members. The biblical idea of giving 10 percent received the response, "My money is mine. Why should I give it away?"

The Bible's answer is Psalm 24:1, "The earth is the LORD's, and everything in it, the world, and all who live in it; for he founded it upon the seas and established it upon the waters." We and our wealth belong to God.

God emphasizes that same principle when he divides up the Promised Land. The land belongs to him. He calls us his people as his rent-free renters to take care of our income in gratitude to him as our Creator and Provider.

Bible Discussion Questions:

1. Read 2 Corinthians 8 and 9. How different is Paul's teaching from ordinary human thinking? What are your responses to the above seven motives for giving? Explain.
2. Give three reasons why we should give at least a tenth of our income? To what causes should we give? Why? With what motives should we give? Explain.

* * *

One Step on Our Journey with Jesus: Decide to plan a budget that puts giving at least ten percent of your income to spiritual causes first, paying off your debts second, and spending it third in using the income with which God has blessed you. Always remember that it's God's income, not yours. You only manage it for him.

* * *

God gives us spiritual progress on our journey

with Jesus by moving us ...

Chapter Four: *From* old giving up on life *to* new giving in to God

4. From old giving up on life:

Keith Drury's fourth temptation of old age is giving up on life and waiting for death. He writes, "Middle age people like to imagine old age as a wonderful time of rest and fun. For some it is, but for many older people, it is harder than that. Betty Davis once quipped, 'Old age is no place for sissies,' reminding us that it's no cake walk for many...." The body just wears out, for some sooner than for others.

For example, memory fades "like the husband watching TV who said, 'Isn't that the fellow—you know that fellow, what's-his-name?'.... The wife responded, 'No, that's the other guy.'"

When our bodies and brains begin wearing out, we're tempted to give up doing anything significant as we wait for the grave. Perhaps, that futile thinking is the source of many instances in which a spouse kills a loved one when the future looks bleak. It may also be the basis of many old-age suicides.

Keith continues, "When offered opportunities to serve in the church or in the community, they sigh, 'Nah, I took my turn; let others do that now.' This is how old folks surrender to the joyless waiting room of death."

The writer of the Book of Ecclesiastes describes the meaninglessness of life without God "under the sun." In chapter twelve, he advises young people, "Remember your Creator in the days of your youth before the days of trouble come and the years approach when you say, 'I find no pleasure in them'" (verse one). For some, old age is a time "when men are afraid of the heights and of dangers in the streets; when the almond tree blossoms and the grasshopper drags himself along and desire no longer is stirred. Then man goes to his eternal home and mourners go about the streets.... 'Meaningless! Meaningless!' says the Teacher. 'Everything is meaningless!'" (verses 5, 8). The writer's point is that if we divorce our life from God, it is futile, and we might as well give up on it as we grow older.

When disappointments and losses pile up over a long lifetime, we can feel depressed or discouraged. In Psalms 42 and 43, the writer grieves about being away from the place of worship and longs to be in the temple praising God with his people (Psalm 42:1-4). If only people today would hunger for worship centered in God's Word as a "deer pants for streams of water" (verse one).

Anyway, the psalmist asks himself, "Why are you downcast, O my soul? Why so disturbed within me?" He recognizes that he's depressed about his exile from group worship in the temple, where God's special presence is. Then, he continues with his pep talk to his soul, "Put your hope in God, for I will yet praise him, my Savior and my God" (42:5).

He then expresses his feelings openly in a lamenting or complaining prayer, "I say to God my Rock, 'Why have you forgotten me? Why must I go about mourning, oppressed by the enemy? My bones suffer mortal agony as my foes taunt me, saying to me all day long, "Where is your God?"'" (42:9). Here, we see an honest expression like the ones in other psalms and in the Book of Job.

One preacher I heard said that such expressions are mistakes, and another one said that the Psalmist is "whining."

Well, God inspired his whole Word, not just the parts that agree with our thinking. The truth is that our culture suppresses open, public, tearful expressions of grief. The result is that our grief often becomes depression, a disease that makes people feel as though they are stuck in a deep, dark hole.

Thus, as we travel the sometimes rough path toward God's final glory, he wants to move us ...

4. <u>**To new giving in to God:**</u>

Fulfilling God's retirement calling

I am seventy years old at this writing. My parents both died in their seventies. My prayer as a writer, a career that God gave me when I retired at almost sixty-six years old, is that if God will give me at least twenty more years of productivity in my fourth career, I will write many more books so that God can bless many more readers. Because God clearly called me to write Christian books in retirement, I am busy writing, revising, and promoting books that I feel God wants me to write to honor my Creator and Rescuer and to benefit many people.

Similarly, one important factor in approaching old age is discovering God's calling for you during that time. Persistent prayer for God's direction is the way to avoid giving up on life and instead giving in to God while growing older. It may also involve taking classes for that calling, which often does not involve getting more income. In addition, God's calling may involve volunteering for worthwhile causes for which God has prepared us with life experiences.

I know older folks, for example, who fix up old donated clocks, appliances, and bicycles for a thrift shop, and others who make quilts for children and adults who are poor or in need.

However, why should we look for God's calling as we age?

The answer is in God's Word, the Bible. In Ephesians 4:1, prisoner Paul wrote, "As a prisoner for the Lord, then, I urge you to live a life worthy of the calling you have received [as believers]." Paul's calling under house arrest in Rome was to share the gospel with people whom God sent to him.

Our calling as Christians is also to share Jesus with acquaintances-becoming-friends near us. (See my book *Doubtbusters! God Is My Shrink!* as a model for friendship outreach.)

But how do we find God's specific calling in retirement? In my case, God prepared me while I was "running away" from a call to the ministry as I chose to be an English teacher with an English master's degree, when I learned to write well, and a sales manager. God also prepared me by making me a pastor in seven churches for twenty-seven years and then giving me a vision for writing. My observation is that God amazingly led me into the right careers during my rebellion, even though I didn't ask him for guidance, in order to prepare me to be a writer in retirement!

We all have the calling to witness to family, friends, and others near us what God has done in our lives (Acts 1:8). Ask him for his Spirit-filling, courage, opportunities to witness, and his words to speak to be his agent of spiritual blessing. God will then benefit other Christians and the younger generation as you share your spiritual experiences.

Think about the worthwhile activities that you could do in old age. For which ones has God given you a passion? How has God prepared you with education and experiences for that possible involvement? It doesn't matter whether you will be paid for your actions, because you will be serving your God, not humans.

Old Testament references to God's choice of us

Why should we feel that our lives in old age are worthwhile? Psalm 33 is a call for all humans to praise the all-powerful Creator of everything, "By the word of the LORD were the heavens made, their starry host by the breath of his mouth.... Let all the earth fear the LORD; let all of the people of the world revere him" (verses 6,8).

Then, the psalmist shares God's special choice of his own people, "Blessed is the nation whose God is the LORD, the people he chose for his inheritance.... But the eyes of the LORD are on those who fear him, on those whose hope is in his unfailing love ..." (verses 12,18). God chooses Israel during the Old Testament. He calls his chosen people there to attract the nations of the world to truly trust in him.

However, Israel fails to be attractive by wandering after false gods and resisting God's call to be his agents of blessing to the nations (Genesis 12:2,3). (See, for example, the Book of Jonah.)

A large number of believers think that the people of God today are only the Jews. However, the New Testament, especially in Paul's writings, says very clearly that all believers in the 3-in-1 God are "children of Abraham" (Romans 4 and Galatians 3). First of all, God's choice of the people of God involves his selection of the visible nation of Israel in the Old Testament as well as the international church in the New Testament era.

Second, his more selective choice causes the rescue of true believers within Israel and the church, Israel's successor. In 1 Kings 19:18, God reassures Elijah that he is not the only believer left among God's people, but that there are still 7,000 Israelites who "have not bowed down to Baal."

Another Old Testament passage (Isaiah 41:8,9) clearly quotes God, who describes his choice of Israel in contrast with idol-worshipers, "But you, O Israel, my servant, Jacob, whom I have chosen, you descendants of Abraham my friend. I took you from the ends of the earth, from its farthest corners I called you.... So do not fear, for I am with you; do not be dismayed, for I am your God. I will strengthen you and help you. I will uphold you with my righteous right hand" (Isaiah 41:8,9a,10). Thus, God chooses spiritual "descendents of Abraham," who are all true believers today, according to the New Testament, as we have seen.

Therefore, our trust in the only true God can take to heart God's call not to fear growing old and dying because he is with us as our God.

Paul's passages about God's selection of us

Next, for God's more selective choice in the New Testament, we go to Ephesians 1:3-14. In that passage, Paul, under the Holy Spirit's inspiration, gives us a mind-boggling, but true glimpse into the shape of God's plans before he made any of the stuff with which all of us are familiar, including matter itself. Paul begins in verse three with his praise for God's human-mind-boggling decisions: "Praise be to the God and Father of our Lord Jesus Christ, who has blessed us in the heavenly realms with every spiritual blessing in Christ. For he chose us in him before the creation of the world to be holy and blameless in his sight. In love he predestined us for adoption to sonship through Jesus Christ...."

One might respond to this passage, "Wait a minute, Paul! You're saying that all of us believers are already in the "heavenly realms" receiving God's blessings and that God chose us before he made anything (verse 4)?! Have you gone off your rocker?" Paul would calmly answer, "Yes, God has revealed those amazing truths to me. No, I'm still safely on my rocker. God is great, isn't he?"

Then, we submit to God's amazing Word by admitting with Paul, "Yes, he certainly is!" This truth is for our comfort as we experience true, growing faith. It is also God's challenge to spread the good news about Jesus Christ so that other chosen people, whoever they are, will believe.

In Ephesians 1:3, Paul writes his wonderful praise for the one true God's many amazing spiritual blessings given to us. The original Greek shows that the word translated "praise" in that verse is similar to the English word *eulogy*, which came from that Greek word. It means to say something good about a person or thing, for example, at a funeral.

As a result, Paul wrote his favorable saying about God. In fact, he seems to be very excited about this truth. How do I know? He uses the word for blessing or praise three times in verse 3. I paraphrase, "I praise the Father of Jesus because he has praised us with spiritual praises!" A person might respond, "I didn't do anything to earn God's praise." That true observation about all of us is exactly Paul's point in saying something good about God.

As a result, all of his gifts are free as his praises to us as his creatures. If that truth doesn't thrill your gizzard, I don't know what will! And our gizzards need thrilling sometimes, especially in the downtimes of old age when we experience the weaknesses of these bodies that wear out. How can we possibly feel worthless in old age in the light of that truth revealed by our awesome God?

Notice also that not only does God consider our position as believers to be in heaven now, but before he made anything, "he chose us in him [Jesus Christ] before the creation of the world" and "he predestined us for adoption" (verses 4 and 5). The original words for "chose" and "predestined" simply mean "selected" and "decided in love with powerful authority ahead of time," respectively.

People often discount this passage because they say that Paul is being fatalistic here. That is, they imagine that he doesn't take into account human responsibility. I strongly disagree. If you tend to feel that way, you should also read Ephesians 4, 5, and 6, where Paul describes Christians' full responsibility to grow in commitment and obedience to the 3-in-1 God. He accepts and rescues us freely, as he describes in chapters 1-3, and strengthens us for holy living.

Thus, how can we give up meaningful living in retirement when we know that God values us so much that he picked us out of humanity before he created anyone?

Other New Testament passages about God's selection of us

You might also note in Acts 2:38 Peter's call for the diverse Jews at the Pentecost feast, who consent to Jesus' crucifixion, to "repent and be baptized... in the name of Jesus Christ for the forgiveness of your sins." Repentance by changing our whole lives is also our full responsibility as our response to Jesus' free rescue by way of his life, death, and resurrection.

Also, if you go back to Acts 2:23, you will see that Peter says to those same people, "This man [Jesus] was handed over to you by God's deliberate plan and foreknowledge; and you, with the help of wicked men, put him to death by nailing him to the cross." Both truths—God's plan to rescue us freely *and* our full responsibility to trust and obey him—are found in this verse and taught in the Bible generally. The amazing fact is that God the Father is ready to forgive those who agree to the death of Jesus, his well-loved Son! Our Father is certainly very different from our fallible, physical fathers!

Therefore, God wants us to submit the fallen logic of our puny minds to God's higher, unlimited logic and admit that the Bible teaches both truths. We also need to accept the fact that the Bible doesn't solve what we may think may be contradictions (for example, how sin entered a perfect creation). God's logic is above and beyond our comparatively feeble reasoning powers.

Anyway, Paul writes that before creation, the one only God—the Father through the second Person, later to become Jesus, by the power of the third Person, the Holy Spirit—marks out in love those who will trust him ages later. His purpose is to rescue us from the depths of destruction into which we are born.

What an amazing stop we are making on our trip toward Jesus' final deliverance!

The passage in Ephesians chapter one continues with an exciting description of the gifts that the mysterious, revealed Creator heaps on us in this life as we trust personally in him through Jesus by the Spirit's power.

Another inspired passage about God's choice is Romans 8:29, 30, where Paul has just shown that the Holy Spirit "cleans up" our prayers and that God arranges every event for the good of all believers. Paul writes, "For those God foreknew he also predestined ..." (verse 29). People who study God have disputed this verse for a long time. Many of them contend that Paul meant to write that God knew beforehand about believers' decisions to trust personally in Jesus and the 3-in-1 God. I respectfully differ with that interpretation, because the text says that God foreknew *them*, not that he only knew *about* them and their decisions.

Why is that fact important? This discussion has a bearing on the tremendous comfort that true Christians experience while secure in the arms of Jesus forever (John 6:35-39; 10:28). In other words, Paul's point is that God *loves us* before his creative work begins.

In the Bible, persons' "knowing" each other involves a close, personal relationship—Genesis 3:20; 18:19 ["have chosen"]; John 10:27. In other words, God picks believers out of the crowd of humanity in love long before we are born in order to make us true believers as his lovely, loved, and loving friends.

However, if you think that these teachings water down human freedom, please read Romans 12-16, where Paul points out believers' responsibility to the God to whom they belong, as he often does in the last parts of his letters. He writes that they need to grow more and more like Jesus in God's powerful, free rescue that Paul describes in the first eleven chapters.

These two aspects of God's deliverance through Jesus by the Holy Spirit are called the "already" and the "not yet" of the Good News. We are "already" perfect in *principle* from God's point-of-view as our Judge, but "not yet" perfect in *practice* because of Jesus' death. These two passages point to the wonderful, comforting teaching that the only true God already plans true believers' rescue long before we even need to be rescued and that he plans to hug us forever! However, they aren't comforting to fakers.

The need to surrender our old age to God

In fact, because God has rescued our lives freely (Romans 1-11), our calling is to offer our "bodies as living sacrifices, holy and pleasing to God—this is your spiritual act of worship. Do not conform any longer to the pattern of this world, but be transformed by the renewing of your mind. Then you will be able to test and approve what God's will is—his good, pleasing, and perfect will" (Romans 12:1, 2). God's will expressed through Paul here is our need to surrender to God as we approach and experience old age.

How can we offer our lives to him? We can offer persistent prayers of surrender about our older years until he leads us to his will for that time. We can also search the Scriptures for his guidance.

For example, more of Paul's inspired advice that we can apply to old age is in Galatians 5:13, 14, 16, "You...were called to be free. But do not use your freedom to indulge the sinful nature; rather, serve one another in love. The entire law is summed up in a single command: Love your neighbor as yourself.... So I say, live by the Spirit, and you will not gratify the desires of the sinful nature."

We can learn several principles about our old-age activities from these verses:

(1) Our freedom in old age is not to be used for ourselves but for God with the guidance of the Holy Spirit through Jesus' powerful victory. Our freedom is never completely free. When fallen people like Adam and Eve want to be free of God, they become enslaved to Satan their whole lives. However, when Jesus' life, death, and resurrection set us free, we become God's adopted children who serve him willingly, gratefully, joyfully, and lovingly.

(2) Giving ourselves to selfish pleasure in old age is not God's freedom but, at least partially, slavery to self and Satan.

(3) God's call to freedom in Jesus is to joyful service to our families, friends, church, and community that God has put near us.

(4) Living by the Spirit is a matter of surrendering to him, our Father, and Jesus, who together are our one true Ruler.

(5) Such victorious living in our old age requires rejection of the sinful nature that still resides within us. Ask God daily what old-nature attitudes and actions are still present in your life. Prayer is necessary every day so that God will replace our sinful nature qualities with the new-nature qualities that he has given us because of Jesus' mighty victory.

God's call to share our life's story

I know a man who was given only a few months to live three years ago! He has a lot of physical problems, including lung and heart ailments, that have confined him to a wheelchair. When I visited him recently, I asked him what keeps him going. He said, "My time isn't up yet. I still have things to do. God has called me to be a witness to hospice and hospital nurses and other people that he sends me." He is a wheelchair witness to God's truth.

God has called all of us to that vocation before and in retirement. How ready are we to be used as his agents as long as he gives us a good mind, no matter how weak our bodies get?

In Acts 1:8, Jesus says to his followers and to us just before he returns to heaven, "But you will receive power when the Holy Spirit comes on you; and you will be my witnesses …" close at home and throughout the world. That verse presents our reason to testify to

God's truth and experiences to nearby people and to give generously for the spread of the Good News to the nations.

On the one hand, the person who says that God doesn't call most of us to be evangelists is right. On the other hand, God calls us to share God's work in our lives and our belief in him with other people as we give him all of the credit.

How has he blessed you throughout your life? Appropriately share those blessings with people near you by humbly giving him all of the credit, because you didn't deserve his heaped, heavenly, good gifts.

During a sleepless summer night in 2007 more than a year before my retirement, a clear idea came to me that I was to write a book about my friendship with a fictional agnostic named Joe Smith. I believe that it was God who was that specific. Thus began my retirement writing career. God's calling for your old-age activities may not be that dramatic, but if you pray for his guidance, he will give it.

F.B. Meyer once confided to his friend F.A. Robinson of Toronto, "I do hope my Father will let the river of my life go flowing fully until the finish. I don't want it to end in a swamp."

Some people think that their older lives are a desert of despair.

However, our old age can be full of meaning when we focus on God and learn from his Word about the value he puts on our lives, even as we age.

When we live in God's great grace, we can sing "Jesus Loves Me" in the following way:

"Jesus loves me, this I know,

Though my hair is white as snow;

Though my sight is growing dim,

Still he bids me trust in him.

Yes, Jesus loves me; yes, Jesus loves me;

yes, Jesus loves me; the Bible tells me so.

Though my steps are, oh, so slow,

With my hand in his I'll go.

On through life let come what may,

He'll be there to lead the way.

When the nights are dark and long,

In my heart he puts a song,

Telling me in words so clear,

"Have no fear, for I am near."

When my work on earth is done

And life's victories been won,

He will take me home above

To the fullness of his love. (C.D. Frey in *The Bible Friend*)

Bible Discussion Questions:

1. Read Galatians chapter five. State in your own words the ways in which we can remove the old sinful nature and put on the new nature in our lives. Which old-nature qualities do present-day Christians have the most trouble removing? Explain.

2. Which new-nature qualities or fruit (Galatians 5:22,23) do you want to develop the most? Why? How can we grow them? Explain.
3. How does prayer enter into this process of taking off old sinful qualities and putting on new godly qualities? Explain.
4. How can God use the prayer process to help us feel worthwhile in old age?

* * *

<u>One Step on Our Journey with Jesus:</u> "Be bolder growin' older" by persistently asking God to show you the worthwhile activities in which he wants you to be involved until he shows you his will. Then, do them prayerfully to honor him.

* * *

God wants us to progress on our plodding pathway …

Chapter Five: *From* feeling abandoned *to* feeling God's powerful presence

5. From feeling abandoned

Keith Drury writes, "Older people are the castaways of a society that is bent on measuring a person's worth by their present contributions. When few people come to see them, loneliness is old people's most frequent visitor…. Feeling abandoned, they are tempted to hold their own pity party: '*Nobody cares anymore—they're just waiting for me to die.*' They might even wonder if God has abandoned them. Surrendering to feeling abandoned is a besetting temptation of old age."

My angry depression and feelings of abandonment

In my subconscious life, my anger at God for permitting our son's death and other losses in my life blocked my sense of God's closeness. Perhaps, older folks' feeling of abandonment by other people and by God may stem from their unresolved grief and/or depression.

An Internet article on the web site www.everydayhealth.com about ten warning signs of depression used to fit me and does fit many older people:

"People with depression do not all have the same symptoms, but they may include:

Sadness. When feeling sad is a symptom of depression, it may include feeling hopeless and empty. You may find that no matter how hard you try, you just can't control your negative thoughts....

Guilt. People with severe depression may feel that they are worthless and helpless. They may even experience their depression as a sign of weakness and can be overly self-critical.

Irritability. This depression symptom may cause you to feel angry, anxious, or restless. Men who are seriously depressed often express their depression through aggression or reckless behavior.

Mental symptoms. If you have trouble concentrating, making decisions, or remembering details, these could be symptoms of depression. People with depression may feel that their thought processes have slowed down.

Physical symptoms. People with depression often have aches and pains, headaches, or digestive problems that do not have any other medical cause and do not respond to treatment.

Loss of energy. If you have depression, you may feel tired all the time....

Loss of interest. A common depression symptom is loss of interest in pleasurable activities....

Sleep changes. Waking up too early in the morning, not being able to fall asleep, or sleeping too much can all be symptoms of depression.

Appetite changes. Changes in eating habits due to depression can result in eating too much or too little.... Some people experience a loss of interest in food, while for others food becomes a way of compensating for feelings of depression.

Suicidal thoughts. Having thoughts of harming yourself is a serious symptom of depression and always needs to be taken seriously. If you're thinking about suicide, you need to get help immediately." (author unknown)

Thankfully, I never had suicidal thoughts, though I can see why depressed people consider taking their own lives. Instead, God gave me such a strong call to the ministry that I felt driven to find out what was wrong with me and to seek God's healing, which he gave me by grace, in order to return to the ministry.

The www.everydayhealth.com article ends with this very important observation, "If you have some of these classic symptoms of depression and the symptoms are severe and have lasted more than a few weeks, you should seek help. The best place to start is with your doctor."

Some old-age humor

A web site www.sticksite.com describes old age in an exaggerated way:

> Your little black book contains only names ending in M.D.
>
> You get winded playing chess.
>
> You look forward to a dull evening.
>
> Forget the health food; I need all the preservatives I can get.
>
> When you fall down, you wonder what else you can do while you're down there.
>
> You're getting older when you get the same sensation from a rocking chair that you once got from a rollercoaster.
>
> You sit in a rocking chair and can't get it going.
>
> Your knees buckle and your belt won't.
>
> You just can't stand people who are intolerant.
>
> The best part of the day is over when the alarm clock goes off.
>
> Your back goes out more often than you do.
>
> You have too much room in your house but not enough in your medicine cabinet.
>
> You sink your teeth into a steak and they stay there.
>
> You decide to procrastinate but never get around to it.
>
> You know that you're getting old when everything either dries up or leaks.
>
> There are three signs of old age. The first is memory loss. I forget the other two.

The cardiologist's diet: If it tastes good, spit it out.

I'm so old that I can laugh, cough, sneeze, and pee all at the same time.

These humorous exaggerations all have an element of truth. No wonder older people often feel abandoned and lonely.

Loneliness in old age

At www.freebiblestudyguides.org, a lesson about loneliness poses the problem. Loneliness "is a challenge we all face to some extent, and many people have experienced deep and painful loneliness." Many songs have expressed loneliness, "Are you lonesome tonight?" "I'm so lonesome I could die," and "Only the lonely know the way I feel tonight. Only the lonely know this feeling."

The following "senior citizen's version" of "Are You Lonesome Tonight?" expresses a little bit of the old-age loneliness in a humorous way:

Are you lonesome tonight?
Does your tummy feel tight?
Did you bring your Mylanta and Tums?

Does your memory stray
To that sunny day
When you had all your teeth and your gums?

Is your hairline receding?
Your eyes growing dim?
Hysterectomy for her,
And it's prostate for him.

Does your back give you pain?
Do your knees predict rain?
Tell me, dear, are you lonesome tonight? (www.sticksite.com)

The writer of www.freebiblestudies.org advises us, "First of all, please don't feel you are weak or weird because you feel lonely.... Also, remember that God wants to be your best friend—he wants to you to talk with him about everything. And as your relationship with God becomes stronger and more intimate, you will feel less loneliness."

Consider the following testimony by a recent widow:

"On January 5, I discovered what true loneliness is. You see, on that day, my husband of over thirty-seven years died. On that day, I felt as if I had died; yet, here I was still alive. There was a huge void in my life. Since I was still alive, I knew that it meant that I needed to go on. In order to do that, I began to look around our congregation. I saw many widows and widowers. There were also many other members who, for one reason or another, were alone. As much as I missed the conversations with my husband, I soon realized that perhaps these others might be starved for conversation. So I came up with a plan. Whenever I felt lonely, I would call someone. Hearing the voice of a friend has helped me."

Her tips for feelings of loneliness follow:

1. Pick up the phone and call someone.
2. Send a card to someone.
3. Visit someone, especially those who are homebound or in a nursing home.

Biblical loneliness

Sometimes we feel that God has abandoned us in our losses, especially as we approach old age. The psalmist David in Psalm 22:1 expresses the same feeling as his enemies gather around him, "My God, my God, why have you forsaken me?" In Mark 15:34, Jesus expresses a similar temptation on the cross as he quotes David. Jesus' enemies are closing in around him like David. As a result, Jesus sympathizes with older folks' feelings of abandonment.

The writer to the Hebrews (4:14-16) says as much: "Seeing then that we have a great High Priest who has passed through the heavens, Jesus the Son of God, let us hold fast our confession. For we do not have a High Priest who cannot sympathize with our weaknesses, but was in all points tempted as we are, yet without sin. Let us therefore come boldly to the throne of grace, that we may obtain mercy and find grace to help in time of need."

Therefore, Satan tempts Jesus on the cross to give in to loneliness, but Jesus also exclaims later to his heavenly Father, "Into your hands I commit my spirit" before he dies. I believe that the Father's justice against our sins and Jesus' expression of the temptation of loneliness are part of the meaning of the three-hour deep darkness leading to Jesus' death. The temptation crosses his mind, but he finds comfort in his Father's approval and protection.

In addition, that conclusion fits the title of this book as God calls us through him to be bolder and more persistent in prayer for God's mercy and grace to enable us to experience his presence all of the time. When we sense God's closeness to listen to our prayers all the time, we pray more for his power to lead us. We can also look around for other people near us with whom we can have fellowship and to whom we can share God's blessings in our lives.

More old-age humor

The web site www.sticksite.com has the following parodies on eight games for older folks:

1. Sag, you're it.
2. Hide and go pee.
3. Twenty questions shouted into your good ear.
4. Kick the bucket.
5. Red Rover, Red Rover, the nurse says bend over.
6. Musical recliners.

7. Simon says something incoherent.
8. Pin the toupee on the bald guy.

As God guides along his path toward his final future, he wants to move us...

5. <u>To feeling his powerful presence:</u>

Overcoming loneliness even when we are alone

Our old-age changes can make us feel as if God and people have abandoned us. I'm sure that younger people sometimes shy away from visiting us because our deteriorating health and physical slowness remind them that some day they will have to deal with old age. Sometimes, people can't face human weakness.

However, God has no human self-centeredness. If we have true faith in our heavenly Father through Jesus Christ's death and resurrection, he is always near us and within us by way of the Holy Spirit. In spite of our lonely feelings, that one true God is with us all the time. Jesus says to his followers after he calls us to "make disciples of all nations.... And surely I am with you always, to the very end of the age" (Matthew 28:19, 20).

Jesus promises to be with you through all of your old-age slips and stumbles on the slippery street toward God's fabulous, final future. He wants to pick you up and use you to be his blessing to people around you. As is often the case, the evil one uses our emotions to deceive us into feeling abandoned.

Furthermore, Jesus knows your pain, since he suffered the burden of your sins' guilt and the Romans' physical flogging and pounded nails on Good Friday.

What hope can we have in our aloneness?

We must recognize the difference between being alone and lonely. We can be alone without being lonely. How? Paul under God's inspiration writes about widows, "The widow who is really in need and left all alone puts her hope in God and continues night and day to pray and to ask God for help. But the widow who lives for pleasure is dead even while she lives" (1 Timothy 5:5, 6). Notice the contrast between a person who constantly and persistently prays as she focuses on God and the one who lives a *selfistic* life. The major difference is between being alive or dead to God. Being alive to God must result in our constant praying.

Jesus teaches us about persistent prayer in a parable about the persistent widow (Luke 18:1-8) to show his disciples "that they should always pray and not give up" (verse one). We don't often have Jesus' commentary about a parable's meaning, but Luke gives it so that we will not miss it. A widow persistently seeks justice from an unjust judge, who finally gives it to her because of her perseverance. Jesus concludes his parable in verse seven, "And will not God bring about justice for his chosen ones, who cry out to him day and night?" How much more than an unjust judge will the perfect, just Judge shower his good gifts on us when we persist in prayer with requests that agree with his will?

God's answer comes as Hebrews 13:5 commands us, "Let your conduct be without covetousness; be content with such things that you have. For he himself said, 'I will never leave you nor forsake you.'"

God's New Testament "Ten Commandments" in the Book of James

Additionally, James 4:7-10 gives us ten commands, "Submit yourselves, then, to God. Resist the devil and he will flee from you. Draw near to God and he will draw near to you. Cleanse your hearts, your sinners, and purify your hearts, you double-minded." How? "Grieve, mourn, and wail. Change your laughter to mourning and your joy to gloom. Humble yourselves before the Lord and he will lift you up."

Notice that feeling close to God involves:

1. submitting to his will,
2. resisting Satan,
3. drawing near to God,
4. cleansing our hearts,
5. purifying our hearts,
6. grieving,
7. mourning,
8. wailing,

Bruce Leiter

    9. changing our laughter to mourning,
    10. humbling ourselves before God.

How can we obey all of these requirements? We can fulfill them through confessing, constant, passionate, persistent prayer. Our culture doesn't give us models of open grieving, but God honors such honest expressions of our grief about our losses and sinfulness, as Job and the psalmists show us. When we persist in such lamenting, God will eventually give us his permanent peace and a sense of his presence in our lives. When he comes near us even though we seldom have people near us, we will not feel lonely. Aloneness doesn't have to be loneliness when we walk and talk with the real Ruler of our lives.

Notice God's sure promises in response to our persistent prayers:

1. The devil, who wants us to feel lonely and depressed, will flee from us.
2. God will come close to us with his gift of peace.
3. He will lift us up to use us as his agents of blessing to others.

How can we overcome feelings of anxiety about being alone? 1 Peter 5:6, 7 echoes James 4:8-10, "Humble yourselves, therefore, under God's mighty hand, that he may lift you up in due time. Cast all your anxieties on him, for he cares for you." In other words, prayerfully and openly throw all of your feelings at God, who will take them and give us peace about all of our losses, especially those in old age. People have trouble hearing our anger and anxiety when we share them, but God wants us to share them with him. He's an excellent Listener!

God's promise of victory over loneliness

How do we know that God will help us overcome our loneliness? Listen to God's promise to bless Israel and us in Isaiah 41:9b-10, "I said, 'You are my servant'; I have chosen you and have not rejected you. So do not fear, for I am with you; do not be dismayed, for I am your God. I will strengthen you and help you; I will uphold you with my righteous right hand." If we feel that God is far away from us, we must pray persistently by claiming his promises in this passage often until we feel his powerful presence.

After all, one of Jesus' names is Immanuel, which means "God with us." We need to pray through Jesus to our Father for his closeness and blessings to supply our needs, especially our emotional needs.

Another promise that we can claim is in Psalm 147:1-3, "Praise the LORD. How good it is to sing praises to our God, how pleasant and fitting to praise him! The LORD builds up Jerusalem, he gathers the exiles of Israel. He heals the brokenhearted and binds up their wounds." When we are consumed with loneliness, it's hard to praise God genuinely.

However, we need to shift our focus from our loss of human companionship to the God who has given us many blessings. In this way, we can praise him for his generosity. As a result, God heals us through our re-focusing on his many divine qualities and actions for us as well as our genuine expression of our feelings in prayer.

Our response of faith to God's promises

In addition to our persistent prayers, God calls us to spring into action in grateful obedience. On the one hand, Jesus warns, "Not everyone who says to me, 'Lord, Lord,' will enter the kingdom of heaven, but only he who does the will of my Father who is in heaven" (Matthew 7:21). He then describes disobedient ones' claim to have done many spectacular actions for him. However, he says to them (7:23), "I never knew you. Away from me, you evildoers!"

Thus, the most important consideration in our seeking God's blessings is our need for a personal relationship with Jesus. Knowing him doesn't just mean understanding a lot of facts about him, but it also means accepting him into our lives as our Friend and Leader on a personal level. Of course, he loves us, but how much do we love him? That close relationship that he wants with us is the covenant friendship that he establishes with us by promising to bless us.

Our response is to pledge our devotion to him by serving other people's needs. Loving prayer and actions for God and for the benefit of other people are our responsibilities that we want to accomplish by the Holy Spirit's power because of our thankfulness for his loving blessings.

In John 14:23, Jesus answers Judas Iscariot's question about Jesus' showing himself only to his followers, "If anyone loves me, he will obey my teaching. My Father will love him, and we will come to him and make our home with him." He then promises the Holy Spirit as our Comforter or Counselor. The Holy Spirit is our Friend-Lawyer who points us to our Father and Jesus as our Source of power and strength to follow him in love.

Incidentally, this kind of love between God and us is, at heart, our personal daily decision to obey him, not primarily a feeling. It is God's free gift in our lives; we can claim no credit for obeying God, who has established his covenant or personal relationship with us. As Jesus says, he and the Father make their home with us in his committed love.

Note also God's observation in Proverbs 12:25, "An anxious heart weighs a man down, but a kind word cheers him up." We can be God's agents of joy in other people's lives by visiting with them and listening to them. If we shift our attention from ourselves and our losses and look outward to other struggling people, God will bless us with his strength.

The anonymous author of www.freebiblestudyguides.org gives us ways to reach out to others:

1. Direct your attention outward to others rather than thinking excessively about self.
2. Determine that you can control your own attitudes and emotions. Ask God for his Spirit of love and joy (Galatians 5:22).
3. Be friendly! Smile! Laugh! Positive attitudes and emotions are contagious and will encourage others to want to be around you (Proverbs 18:24). (This advice isn't really in conflict with James chapter four, since we can do our grieving in private prayer while encouraging others with the joy we feel when we focus on God and his greatness.)
4. Go to church and church activities and fellowship with others. Consider their needs and try to encourage them.
5. Participate in various activities. Be involved with others.
6. Volunteer your services to others at church, hospitals, schools, and libraries. Consider visiting a nursing home to cheer up the residents. You will soon have a different perspective on loneliness.
7. Develop a new hobby. Expand your interests. Engage in conversations focusing on other people's interests.

Be Bolder Growin' Older

8. Use technology to be in touch. E-mails, Facebook, and Twitter can be fun ways to interact with others.
9. Establish a circle of friends that you talk to on the phone. Include people who may be lonely.
10. If you have depression and loneliness that you cannot pull out of, please seek help through counseling to get in touch with the cause of your feelings. Remember, depression is a disease for which we must get help. Then, we can know better how to pray.

Bible Discussion Questions:

1. Look at all of the quoted Bible passages in this chapter. Which ones are most helpful for your Christian life? Why?
2. What do you think about James' ten commandments (4:7-10)? Which of them are the hardest for present-day Christians to fulfill? Why do you think our culture doesn't allow us to grieve, mourn, and wail publicly? Explain.
3. In biblical times, people who lost a loved one hired professional mourners who would come to their house to mourn with tears to help them grieve openly. How do you feel about that practice? Explain.
3. How do you feel when someone cries in your presence? Why?
4. Which of the above ten suggestions for overcoming loneliness will be most useful to you? Why?

***

<u>**One Step on Our Journey with Jesus:**</u> **Let yourself cry persistently and freely in private as you express your loneliness, anger, feeling of abandonment, or other feelings openly and honestly to God. Resolve by God's grace to ask for his guidance to be his agent of blessing in other people's lives.**

***

Now, as we travel toward God's final kingdom,

he enables us to move...

Chapter Six: *From* bitterness *to* permanent peace about life

6. From bitterness about life

Internet observations about grumpiness

Keith Drury in his Internet article "Ten Temptations of Old Age" observes, "Most of us know someone who became 'a bitter old man.' It can happen to women, too. Sometimes it even happens to 'great leaders' who end poorly and leave a sour taste in the memories of those who remember them. How does this bitterness happen?"

Keith describes a couple possible causes that he has heard from old people. On the one hand, some middle aged people have high expectations for an active, healthy old age and are bitter when they actually experience poor health and limitations. On the other hand, some older folks perceive that church leaders want old folks' money but not their advice.

Well, I know from experience that bitterness often comes from a deeper cause. Psychologists tell us that we are born with two emotions—fear and anger expressed by flight and fight. Fear retreats from the object of fear, while anger wants to attack its object.

The web site www.sticksite.com points up the ironic reverses of old age, especially some people's bitter dissatisfaction:

> I'm very good at opening childproof caps...with a hammer.
> I'm usually interested in going home before I get to where I'm going.
> I'm not really grouchy. I just don't like traffic, waiting, crowds, lawyers, loud music, unruly kids, Jenny Craig and Toyota commercials, barking dogs, politicians, and a few other things I can't seem to remember right now.
> I'm wrinkled, saggy, lumpy, and that's just my left leg.
> I'm wondering, if you're only as old as you feel, how could I be alive at 150?
> I'm a walking storehouse of facts. I just lost the key to the storeroom door."

The sources of my personal bitterness

For the first forty-three years of my life, I was a bitter guy without knowing it. Why was I angry? I'm sure that my anger began in my mother's womb. While I was growing in that supposedly safe place, my parents struggled and stressed out over my three-year-old brother Bobby's leukemia, from which he died when I was two and a half months old. Researchers have demonstrated that family stress affects unborn babies in their mothers' wombs.

I believe that early experience made me sensitive to stress and began my life of anger, which built up like steam in a teakettle unless I somehow opened the valve to let it out. I know that I held that angry steam inside of me.

When I was four or five years old, as I rode my tricycle around the tennis court behind our three-story house in Kirkwood, Missouri, a suburb of St. Louis, I somehow turned a corner too quickly and fell down. I've always been a klutz. I lay bawling on the concrete.

My mother, who was forty when I was born, hustled out of our house, picked me up, dusted me off, and admonished me, "Big boys don't cry!" That unhealthy advice that I accepted from our repressed culture resulted in forty years of repressed anger that increased to bitterness, which I covered up with a smile, and finally to emotional shutdown almost at the end of my seven years of depression.

The symptoms of my bitterness were a loud voice, growing irritability, and an intense, sometimes dominant personality.

Why do we have so many mass shootings in our society? Men like Adam Lanza, often in their twenties, shoot multiple victims like the twenty children and six educators that he shot at Sandy Hook School in Newtown, Connecticut, on December 14, 2012, after he shot his own mother.

From personal experience, I believe that our culture teaches us, especially us men, to swallow our fear and anger. Those emotions build up until they show up later in some way as bitterness or rage (uncontrolled anger).

I was bitter about my brother Bobby's death but also about many other losses in my life. After Bobby died, my mother found comfort in attending and being active in church. My father, on the other hand, stayed home from church and found comfort in his pragmatic, humanistic philosophy of life.

My mother was extremely strict and legalistic like her father, a county judge. Dad was extremely permissive. The result in my life was confused insecurity. Mom would say to Dad, "The boys should clean up their room," but Dad would respond, "I don't think that's important."

In addition, since my father was the permissive one and stayed home from church, we boys wanted to stay home too like Dad. However, my Christian mom with an iron will "dragged" us to church every Sunday, an action for which I will be eternally thankful.

Playground bullies, sensing my insecurity, picked on me. One snowy, winter day, they dragged me, kicking and screaming, out to the snowball field and pelted me mercilessly with dozens of snowballs.

I tried to compensate for my lonely insecurity by being a good, hardworking student to gain the love of my teachers and my parents, both of whom were college graduates back in the 1920s. My mother paid me for good grades, but I never sensed that my studious performance earned me anyone's admiration and love.

Furthermore, our family was emotionally distant from each other. My parents favored my two brothers over me. I was lonely in a family of five.

We lived on a miniature family farm. Dad was a traveling baby-diaper-service manager and salesman and farmed on weekends. He drove a thousand miles all week, while I was stuck with my mom, who ruled according to the "laws of the Medes and Persians." That quote from the Book of Daniel was her favorite phrase when we boys asked why we had to work in the garden, for example. While my brothers loved the farm, I hated the work, especially forking the cow manure out of the flat-roofed barn into the spreader as well as hot haying.

I was angry about my dysfunctional family without knowing it.

The Bible's teachings about anger

The Bible teaches us about anger. God's anger develops very slowly and is far from sinful. It is righteous anger in response to human rebellion.

However, human anger often is self-centered, as mine was. Because we are born thinking that we are the center of the universe, we react with anger and fear when our lives don't go the way we want.

For example, when God rescues 2,000,000 Israelites from hard labor in Egypt with ten miraculous plagues and opens the Red Sea, you'd think that they would put their trust in him and feel constant, grateful joy. However, when the Egyptian chariot army seemingly traps them against the Red Sea, the leaders complain to Moses, "Was it because there were no graves in Egypt that you brought us to the desert to die? What have you done to us by bringing us out of Egypt" (Exodus 14:11)?

Anger and fear often result in sarcastic complaining. Indirectly, they are also angry at the God of their ancestors, who did mighty miracles for them through Moses. Can't he do another one to give them his deliverance, especially since God's fiery pillar leads them there?

"Moses answers the people, 'Stand firm and see the deliverance the LORD will bring you today.... The LORD will fight for you; you only need to be still" (Exodus 14:13a, 14). That observation seems humanly ridiculous, but God is beyond human thought and imagination. When we feel irritated, frustrated, or bitter about our lives, he says that we should take our feelings to him in prayer rather than complaining to others.

Of course, God fights for the Israelites by opening the Red Sea with high water-walls on either side of a dry path and then closing it on the obstinate Egyptians, who brought their punishment on themselves.

The next time the Israelites are in distress from lack of water at Marah, do they learn from their Red Sea experience? "When they came to Marah, they could not drink its water because it was bitter.... So the people grumbled against Moses, saying, 'What are we to drink?'" (Exodus 15:24).

When people complain bitterly about their lives, it may be evidence that anger has built up within them, often from childhood. The Israelites' anger at their Egyptian slavemasters transfers to Moses and indirectly to the God of their rescue to freedom. We humans are often a sorry lot!

In contrast to the people's bitter complaint to Moses, he "cried out to the LORD, and the LORD showed him a piece of wood. He threw it into the water, and the water became sweet" (Exodus 15:25). Did they learn to trust in and pray to the only true God? No! Later, God's just anger is aroused by nine more rebellions. The result is that that whole generation of the community of Israel except for Caleb and Joshua has to die in the desert without reaching the Promised Land because of their angry rebellion.

Moreover, Solomon writes in Proverbs 29:22, "An angry man stirs up dissension, and a hot-tempered one commits many sins."

Also, in Matthew 6:22, Jesus extends the commandment "You shall not murder" to self-centered anger, "Anyone who is angry with his brother will be subject to judgment." Muslims, Mormons, and others have charged that the early church changed the Bible to agree with their ideas, but why then would they change the command not to murder to make it much harder to fulfill? That charge lacks credibility, especially when Jesus calls us in the same Sermon on the Mount to be perfect, avoid judging or condemning people, and love our enemies!

Finally, so that we won't draw the conclusion that expressions of anger are always wrong, Paul in Ephesians 4:26, 27 commands us in the context of putting off the old nature and putting on the new one, "'In your anger do not sin' [Psalm 4:4]. Do not let the sun go down while you are still angry, and do not give the devil a foothold." Paul under God's inspiration warns us against letting our anger fester like an infected wound over a period of time.

Instead, righteous anger purely focuses on God's honor, not ours, and is never directed at people. We can be righteously angry at the selfish murder of unborn infants, while loving and feeling compassion for those fellow sinners who want to take those helpless lives.

More of my personal anger

What else was I angry about, and how did I show it? When Jesus came into my life at the age of sixteen, he filled up my loneliness and insecurity with himself. However, my anger about my childhood remained unexamined. In high school, I finally found some friends. We then made fun of loners and outcasts. My anger showed up in that way.

Many years later when I was a salesman, I met one of the people that we criticized. She was very bitter about our actions. I apologized, but, sadly, she would not accept my apology.

I also expressed my anger by yelling at other drivers for going too slow or cutting me off in traffic. I'm afraid that I wasn't a good example to my wife and children by railing at people in other cars. You see, repressed anger does come out and continues until it is faced and overcome.

When I attended Calvin College with God's clear call to preach his Word, I rebelled against his call because of the required Greek major. Instead, I went into English teaching and acquired an English master's degree. My actions expressed my anger at God's requirement.

When our second child, Keith, came down with leukemia and, after almost three years, died during my last year of teaching, we went through what the psalmists refer to as the "depths." We suffered with Keith and all came down with hepatitis during the winter of 1971-2, I'm sure because of the extreme stress caused by his disease. My bitterness increased greatly because God allowed Keith to die in October 1972.

Seven years of the disease of depression

For seven years after Keith died, I was *relatively* okay. Then, from 1979-1986, I experienced tiredness developing into exhaustion and finally emotional shutdown. I found out later that I had the disease of depression, which for me was buried, bottled-up anger and anxiety because of a heavy load of grief that I tried to cover up with a smile. The depression's most important cause was my anger at God for his plan that allowed Keith's death and other losses in my life.

During my seven-year depression, I became more and more irritable, had trouble remembering details, was angry especially at other drivers, went from fatigue to exhaustion, experienced emotional shutdown, developed sleep apnea, and ate more food—all symptoms of depression.

At the depth of my deep, dark depression, the chronic aches and pains of fibromyalgia suddenly developed on the morning of the fourth Friday in March 1986. My prayers seemed to be bouncing off the ceiling as I felt that God was far away. Of course, he was near me, but I felt abandoned.

God has also allowed people to act in unChristian and unloving ways in my life. What's more, my depression deepened when I had to retire the first time due to that same depression, even though I had a very strong call to the ministry.

You see now why I was a very bitter guy even as a Christian.

Bible Discussion Questions:

1. How do you feel about the author's forty-three years of bitterness? Explain.
2. How is God's anger different from most human anger, for example, the Israelites' anger at Moses and God after they left

Egypt? Why did they get so angry even though they had experienced God's many miracles? Explain.
3. Read Proverbs 29:22, Matthew 6:22, and Ephesians 4:26, 27. What conclusions about human anger do you draw from these passages? Explain.

* * *

One Step on Our Journey with Jesus: If you suspect that you might have some unresolved anger or bitterness but can't remember what the original cause might be, get psychological help to discover what you are *really* angry about. Then, express and confess your anger persistently in prayer until God gives you his peace.

* * *

While we travel Jesus' journey, God wants to move us…

6. To permanent peace about life

God's solution for my bitterness

By God's grace, he used psychological means to get me in touch with my anger at his permitted plan for my life that allowed a number of losses.

As I describe in *Doubtbusters! God Is My Shrink!* God used dramatic psychological means enabling me to get in touch with my anger at him and then healed my depression through a biblical pattern that is not part of our culture—tearful, lamenting prayers. Those persistent prayers over an eight and a half month period resulted in my sense of God's closeness, even while I was mad at him, and in his free gift of eventual, permanent peace about those bitter years! What's more, God got rid of my depression and my buried bitterness!

Since then, every time I get a little tired, I ask God why I'm angry. God gives me an idea about the object of my wrath, and I begin lamenting. I persistently ask God with tears why he has allowed that situation in my life, while confessing my self-centeredness, until he gives me the peace of Philippians 4:6, 7. In this way, he has given me peace about my chronic pain and daily migraines. While he has not taken away the former, he has dramatically relieved my headaches. I praise him for his gift of peace and the relief that he has given me (see *Doubtbusters*).

Biblical lamenting

I have already discussed Job's laments and Psalm 88. Another psalm of lament is Psalm 39. David begins his lament by writing about suppressing his anger, "But when I was silent and still, not even saying anything good, my anguish increased. My heart grew hot within me, and as I meditated the fire burned ..." (verses 2 and 3). David knows that holding in his anger about losses is unhealthy and that the beginning of the solution is to express his feelings, "Then I spoke with my tongue."

However, it's not helpful to dump our emotional baggage in a negative way on other people, especially our family and friends. God can easily hear our anger or bitterness, whereas people often cannot bear those feelings. Also, David will dishonor God by sharing his anger and anxiety with unbelievers.

However, prayer is the outlet, the teakettle valve, for his pent-up fight and flight. In Psalm 39:4-6, he echoes his famous son Solomon in Ecclesiastes with his depressed declaration about life's seeming meaninglessness, "Man is a mere phantom as he goes to and fro: he bustles about but only in vain; he heaps up wealth, not knowing who will get it" (verse 4).

Then, David reveals his reason for expressing his feelings in prayer, "But now, Lord, what do I look for? My hope is in you" (verse 7). David clings to God by expressing his anger about his desperate situation and hoping for his divine Deliverer's rescue. Though this psalm has little positive content, the facts that David hopes for God's triumph and that he focuses his prayer on his God are the positive aspects that we can carry over into our lamenting prayers as we pour out our bitterness and anger to God.

David does not only express his depressed anger, but he also confesses his self-centeredness and asks that God make him a good example to unbelievers who might judge him because of his losses, "Save me from all my transgressions; do not make me the scorn of fools." He also recognizes that God is somehow involved in his struggles, "I was silent; I would not open my mouth, for you are the one who has done this. Remove your scourge from me; I am overcome by the blow of your hand" (verses 9, 10).

Moreover, the Book of Job reveals that God allows but does not cause the sicknesses and other struggles in our lives. Rather, Satan directly causes the deaths of Job's family, his loss of wealth, and his sickness. On the other hand, God limits Satan's attacks. Similarly, in Psalm 39, David knows that his loss is part of God's permissive plan for his life.

The Bible knows nothing about modern secularism that divorces God from everyday life and instead talks about luck, chance, or fate. Rather, Psalm 39 and many other Scriptures acknowledge God's involvement in all of life. For example, in Romans 8:28 after Paul writes that the Holy Spirit assists our prayers, he makes this amazing statement, "And we know that in all things God works for the good of those who love him." God is involved in every detail of our lives for our good. Praise the Lord!

David's lamenting prayers resulting in real relief

David continues to plead tearfully and boldly for God's gift of relief from his distress, "Hear my prayer, O LORD, listen to my cry for help; be not deaf to my weeping. For I dwell with you as an alien, a stranger, as all my fathers were" (Psalm 39:12).

My advice for your prayers is like the pattern of this and other psalms. If you have any unresolved anger or bitterness and find it difficult to forgive other people and, therefore, God for past events, "be bolder growin' older" by expressing your feelings honestly to God in prayer, while confessing your sinfulness in holding onto your grudges.

Another psalm of lament is Psalm 22. David's enemies have surrounded him as he writes (verse 1a), "My God, my God, why have you forsaken me?" On the cross, Jesus quotes these words as the temptation that he feels to question his heavenly Father.

People have said that we must not ask God "Why?" However, my experience has been that such a question is more an expression of my anger than it is asking God for information. Therefore, if you're angry at God's plan for your life and you want to ask him why he has allowed your losses, go ahead and ask him, letting your tears flow, while confessing your selfishness in wanting your plan for your life instead of his. If you feel it, share it with him persistently. He won't run away from you but will instead be very close.

David expresses his desperation, not despair, throughout the psalm. Jesus' suffering fulfills many of the details of his anguish that are also reflected in the Suffering Servant's experience in Isaiah 53, for example, people's mocking him (Psalm 22:6-8) and dividing his garments among them (Psalm 22:18).

By contrast, Psalm 34 expresses the great relief that David feels in praising God for his protective deliverance. He begins, "I will extol the LORD at all times; his praise will always be on my lips. My soul will boast in the LORD; let the afflicted hear and rejoice. Glorify the LORD with me; let us exalt his name together."

Why? "I sought the LORD, and he answered me; he delivered me from all my fears. Those who look to him are radiant; their faces will never be covered with shame. This poor man cried, and the LORD heard him; he saved him out of all his troubles. The angel of the LORD encamps around those who fear him, and he delivers them" (Psalm 34:1-7).

Several comments about Psalm 34:1-7 are necessary:

(1) Notice that David has moved beyond the trials of Psalms 22 and 39 to God's victory.

(2) The result in his life is joyful praise to the God who rescues him.

(3) He resolves to praise and pray to his covenant God all of the time.

(4) David uses the name for his God, LORD or Yahweh, that the God of the perpetually burning bush reveals to Moses in Exodus 3 and 4. Yahweh is God's covenant name as the divine Deliverer in covenant relationship with his loved ones.

(5) Notice also that the only acceptable boasting is in the LORD, not in David's own abilities.

(6) David calls himself "poor," though he has great wealth. We're all poor, that is, in great need of God's emotional healing and blessings that he wants to give us.

(7) Look at the great results in the lives of people whom God carries through the changes of life to provide emotional healing for them. Their faces are "radiant" and without shame because of their God, who later goes through Jesus' extreme suffering and suffocating death in order to free us from our bitterness and anger about our suffering.

New Testament lamenting and personal peace

So that you do not take this lamenting pattern as limited to the Old Testament, let's turn to Philippians 4:4-7: "Rejoice in the Lord always; I will say it again, Rejoice! Let your gentleness be evident to all. The Lord is near. Do not be anxious about anything, but in everything, by prayer and petition, with thanksgiving, present your requests to God. And the peace of God, which transcends understanding, will guard your hearts and your minds in Christ Jesus."

Notice that three commands begin this passage: calls to constant joy, gentleness, and freedom from anxiety. The path to progress in more rejoicing, gentle living, and lack of fear is through prayerful requests. One of those prayers involves lamenting questions that may include "Why?" However, those prayers are to include thanksgiving, a reminder that though bitterness often focuses on our negative circumstances, we still have a lot for which we need to be thankful.

The real result of our persistent prayers will be God's unfathomable peace. It "transcends understanding" because our past certainly has not changed, but God provides us through prayer with an ability to let go of our bitterness and anger about our losses.

After seven and a half months of tearfully expressing my anger that God had allowed so many losses in my life three or four times a week, God removed my depression. After I lamented another month, he gave me the "peace that transcends understanding" of Philippians 4:7 that has been permanent about those first forty-three years of my life. That peace has remained for more than twenty-five years.

I've heard people say that a person never gets over the loss of a child, but I declare to you that God can give you peace from the bitterness and depression that sometimes come with the "golden years," even about such a traumatic loss. His Word promises it in response to our persistent prayers of honest, open lamenting that expresses our true feelings of fear, anger, and bitterness. Claim his Philippians 4:7 promise in prayer for the constant calmness that only he can give you.

How was I different after God gave his gift of peace? I no longer yell at other drivers. Their poor driving became a minor irritation rather than a loud, intense harangue. In fact, my stress-laden, loud voice became a quieter, calmer voice, though my voice still naturally projects. One church member described me as "laid-back," a term that certainly did not describe me before God's gift of permanent peace about the past. See *Doubtbusters! God Is My Shrink!* for God's dramatic, true breakthroughs that eventually gave me his peace.

Since then, the stress of anger has built up again about my chronic pain and daily migraines. I would get tired again, ask God what I was getting depressed about, lament persistently, and receive his peace about those issues. His peace is calm acceptance of my losses as part of his plan for my life. Yes, he is my Shrink in shrinking my bitterness and anger by enabling me to forgive him and other people! He's the Judge, not me!

Bible Discussion Questions:

1. Read Psalm 39, then Psalm 34. Describe in your own words the change in emotions between the two psalms.
2. What value does Psalm 39 have for our Christian lives? Why?
3. Read Philippians 4:4-7. What goals does this passage have for our lives, and what does God promise to give us after persevering prayer? Describe that gift in your own words.
4. How will you put into action the truths of these Bible passages? Explain.

* * *

One Step on Our Journey with Jesus: Examine your life with psychological help, if necessary, for any anger or bitterness about past losses or reverses. Pray perseveringly private prayers that openly express your anger and anxiety about past and present losses and other people's unloving actions. Persist in prayer asking for God's promised, permanent peace until he gives it to you.

***

As we limp during our spiritual tourist trip toward our future resurrection perfection, God wants to move us…

Chapter Seven: *From* old despair *toward* new integrity

7. <u>From old despair</u>

One opinion about old age's view of life

Keith Drury, in his Internet article "The Temptations of Old Age," refers to psychologist Erik Erikson, who "suggested seven challenges humans faced through life, forks in the road where one could take the wrong or right fork. He labeled his final fork for the aged as 'Integrity vs. Despair.' By 'Integrity' he meant an old person who looks back over his life and sees it … largely as worthwhile, e.g., *'I've made some mistakes in my life but my life was worth living.'* The other fork (Despair) is when an old person reflects on life and regrets the way it turned out."

Looking at life God's way

How can we avoid despair and regrets about our lives? The Bible helps us to evaluate our lives rightly with a deeper analysis. On our journey toward our final victory in Jesus, I have already described the Bible's honest view of our human nature. As we look back on our lives, we have to admit that we don't just make mistakes. Instead, we are born rebellious sinners who will answer to the just Judge for all of our selfish desires, feelings, thoughts, attitudes, and actions. We are far from guilt-free about the "mistakes" that we have done.

Chapter one of this book describes Paul's indictment of humanity in Romans chapter one. In the next two chapters, Paul relentlessly builds his case that all people are guilty and worthy of eternal punishment after death.

Then, after Paul restates his case that "Jews and Gentiles alike are all under sin" (Romans 3:9c) and lists many Old Testament passages describing all humans' great guilt (Romans 3:10-18), God's Word says that "all have sinned and fall short of the glory of God ..." (Romans 3:24).

Furthermore, inspired Paul writes in Ephesians 2:1-3, "As for you, you were dead in your transgressions and sins in which you used to live when you followed the ways of this world and of the ruler of the kingdom of the air, the spirit who is now at work in those who are disobedient. All of us also lived among them at one time, gratifying the cravings of our sinful nature and following its desires and thoughts. Like the rest, we were by nature objects of wrath." What a dark view Paul has about our entrance into this world! We can see why some people give in to despair in old age if they only look at this passage.

The Apostle John also shares this dark view of human nature, "If we claim to be without sin, we deceive ourselves, and the truth is not in us" (1 John 1:8).

We have not just made mistakes but have been rebellious sinners from birth. Therefore, at first blush, our lives have been much worse than the view of the person who looks back on his life with integrity by admitting his mistakes but is largely satisfied with it. No, we are much more wicked than we would like to admit.

During the first sixteen years of my life, I was a people-pleasing, Pharisaical "good boy." I tried to be obedient to adult authority in my own strength with a self-centered desire to get other people's approval and love. Yes, I rebelled passive-aggressively against my mother's authority, but I too would have excused those actions as boyish mistakes. In reality, I was an inwardly-rebellious sinner literally on my way to hell and rightly so because I was an "ignorostic" by ignoring God, my Creator.

If we stop here on our travelers' trip, we have every reason to descend to despair as we survey our lives in old age. However, God wants to lift us out of such despair.

One way we can escape despair is found in the context of 1 John 1:8. The inspired Apostle John goes from people's denial of their sinfulness to write, "If we confess our sins, he is faithful and just and will forgive us our sins and purify us from all unrighteousness" (1 John 1:9).

(1) The way to avoid despair about our imperfect lives is prayers of confession. Again, prayer is the key to dealing with and overcoming any despair or escapism about our lives in old age.

(2) God is faithful by replacing his justice with his love for us because of Jesus' victory.

(3) God is just toward us because Jesus as our Substitute becomes the Object of our Father's anger against our sins through his gift of our faith.

(4) God's forgiveness heaps on his unique Son, the crucified Jesus, his right anger against believers. No wonder a period of three hours of deep darkness precedes Jesus' death for us.

(5) God continues to "purify us from all unrighteousness" throughout our lives by way of his Word the Bible, Jesus' death, and the Holy Spirit's cleansing work.

As I write, the Cleveland judge who presided over Ariel Castro's despicable imprisonment and abuse of three women for about a decade has pronounced Castro's sentence of life without parole plus 1,000 years in prison. We are all similarly guilty of many sins, and such a penalty is symbolic of God the Judge's just verdict of eternal punishment on us unless he himself pays the price through Jesus' death as our Substitute on the cross. Such a release can only happen through his free gift of faith or trust in Jesus as the only Path to our Father.

Bible Discussion Questions:

1. Read Romans 1:18–3:19; Ephesians 2:1-3; and 1 John 1:8. How do you feel about your life in the light of these passages? Why can't we believers descend into despair in evaluating our lives?

2. Why is it important to look at our lives in such a negative way? What does Paul's accusation about the human race say about our Creator-Rescuer? What evidence do you see in the news that humanity is thoroughly sinful, as Paul describes?
3. Why do some people feel despair as they evaluate their lives in old age? Explain.
4. Look at 1 John 1:9. What is God saying to you about your life in this verse? Why?

* * *

<u>One Step on Our Journey with Jesus:</u> Persistently confess all of your sinfulness to God in prayer until he gives you peace about your far-from-perfect past. Experience his resulting gift of peace that is focused on him as your peace-giver instead of despair as you look at your life.

* * *

As we lope along the road with Jesus, God nudges us…

7. <u>Toward new integrity</u>

According to Keith Drury's psychologist Erik Erikson, instead of despair, we need integrity to consider our whole lives worthwhile. Well, I have already shown God's opinion that we are lost, dead, and guilty before him when we are born into this world. Such a life is not worthwhile. Then, how should we look at our lives in old age?

We go back to inspired Paul's comments in Romans 3:20, "But now a righteousness from God, apart from law, has been made known, to which the Law and the Prophets testify."

(1) The word "but" provides an amazing contrast to the previous three chapters describing our great guilt.

(2) Paul contrasts human "righteousness" based on following the Law with God's righteousness as his free gift.

(3) God has revealed his righteousness through Jesus. Our choice is between our futile attempts to please God and other people in our own strength or, instead, receiving God's gift of right standing and life only through Jesus' perfect life and death in our place.

(4) The whole Old Testament points forward to God's righteousness coming through Jesus.

Paul continues, "This righteousness comes through faith in Jesus Christ to all who believe. There is no difference, for all have sinned and fall short of the glory of God and are justified freely by his grace that came by Christ Jesus. God presented him as a sacrifice of atonement, through faith in his blood" (Romans 3:22-

25a). Paul goes on to declare that God, the just Judge, sends Jesus to the cross in our place to satisfy his justice toward us.

The result is believers' justification. In other words, Jesus' perfect death takes believers' guilt on himself so that God the Father considers us "not guilty" and right with him as our Creator-Judge. The question is that as we look back on our life, have we attempted to earn God's approval on our own hook? Instead, have we received and accepted Jesus' perfect death in our place?

We can feel old-age despair if we rely on our own right living in our own strength. However, if we depend on and trust in Jesus' right life and death for us, we can have the integrity of joyful praise for his free gift of God the Father's justification in our old age.

As a result, in old age we can rejoice in his powerful presence, enabling us to focus on his grace in freely accepting us. It's not because of any quality in us that he delivers us but solely due to Jesus' many perfections.

Thus, it's not our accomplishments that we celebrate in old age but Jesus' accomplishments for us. In fact, the more we focus on our 3-in-1 God in prayer and praise, being "bolder growin' older," the more we can find his gift of joy instead of the temptation of despair. We revel in God's grace, his free acceptance.

As we revisit Ephesians 2, where Paul paints our sad life's beginning in stillbirth, he uses another of his pivotal "buts" in verse 4, "But because of his great love for us, God, who is rich in mercy, made us alive with Christ even while we were dead in transgressions...." Thus, in old age as we praise God for his love and mercy, he lifts up our whole being from despairing depths to heavenly habits. Notice that we can in no way earn God's approval, though our fallen human nature wants at least some of the credit, just as all of the other religions and cults do.

This stop on our journey with Jesus lifts us up to constant prayer and praise to God rather than navel-gazing at our lives.

Then, Paul summarizes the Good News in Ephesians 2:8-10, "For it is by grace you have been saved, through faith—and this not from yourselves; it is the gift of God—not by works so that no one can boast. For we are God's workmanship, created in Christ Jesus to do good works, which God prepared in advance for us to do." Notice that the word "works" is used in two ways. The first use of "works" (verse 9) is Paul's denial that our own efforts apart from God's powerful grace have any weight with God. Paul's other, more positive use of "works" is in verse 10, where God enables us to do works of gratitude solely to his credit. Grace producing good works apart from any deeds coming from our personal power is foreign to human thinking. Therefore, God shows it to us through Paul in the Bible.

Thus, the integrity that can replace our old-age despair is God's integrity in earning our high position through Jesus Christ.

While I revisit Bible passages from chapter eight's first part, I also want to quote 1 John 1:10, "If we claim we have not sinned, we make him out to be a liar and his word has no place in our lives." If we have selective memory in old age for only our good works or if we dwell on our "mistakes" without admitting that they are sins that offend our divine Judge, we need John's correction of our over-protective view of our lives. We have sinned and are guilty—unless we receive Jesus' perfection in our place.

First John 1:8-10 clearly says that we are guilty sinners, as Jesus and Paul agree, but those verses also declare emphatically that God himself has provided Jesus as the Solution to our dilemma as objects of his anger. What an amazing stop we have on our journey with Jesus toward his final triumph!

Bible Discussion Questions: What does this part of chapter eight say about how we need to interpret Bible passages? In other words, in the first part of this chapter, we considered three parts of the same Bible passages that we examined in this part. How do the contexts of those first passages (Ephesians 2:1-10; Romans 3:1-25a; 1 John 1:8-10) help us understand them more fully? Explain.

* * *

One Step on Our Journey with Jesus: Devote your prayers to include joyful praise for God's free gift of Jesus' perfection in your life as a believer.

* * *

Now, on our joyful journey God wants us to progress ...

Chapter Eight: *From* old doubt *to* new confidence in the God of the Bible

I believe that doubt comes in at least three parts of our lives: our thinking, feeling, and deciding. Keith Drury writes that doubt about God's goodness creeps into old people's lives "when an old person faces pain, abandonment, and death, and [when] their old age did not turn out to be the icing on the cake...." God wants to move us ...

8. <u>From old doubt</u>

God's Word, the Bible, clearly describes his creation of the first man and woman as made in his image and likeness (Genesis 1:26, 27). Human experience made up of our reason, emotions, and will, I believe, dimly reflects God's abilities to think, feel, and decide. However, divine experience with those capabilities is completely foreign to those parts of human experience because of our fall into self-centered sin.

For example, in Isaiah 55:1-7, the prophet describes God's free food and forgiveness in response to our repentance. Then he quotes God in 55:8, 9, "'For my thoughts are not your thoughts, neither are your ways my ways,' declares the LORD. 'As the heavens are higher than the earth, so are my ways higher than your ways and my thoughts than your thoughts.'" Throughout the Bible, divine experience is very different from self-centered human experience.

Thus, God must have inspired the Bible because the human minds that wrote it couldn't have conjured it up.

It seems to me that what we call doubt can arise when we think, feel, and/or decide as we approach or endure old age. That doubt arises from the great difference between divine and human experience. After all, any action that we do without praying is, in reality, doubt in action, since Paul in 1 Thessalonians 5:17 writes God's command, "Pray continually" or "without ceasing" (KJV).

When we are young, we may experience God a little bit, but we tend to let human experience dominate us because we assume that we are invincible. When we get into our twenties and thirties, we are too busy establishing our work and families to experience life the way God does except, perhaps, at church. During middle age, work and our (grand)children consume our lives to keep us from the divine experience. As we retire and move into old age, we either stay very busy with our families with continued good health or we experience health challenges. In any case, at some point, we slow down with more time to think, feel, and decide about our past lives.

Thus, our secular human experience can influence us to make us doubt God at all of our lives' stages. However, during old age, we are particularly vulnerable. An example is Job's life. He is committed to and serving God faithfully. When God allows Satan to take away his possessions and family as God's test, Job grieves but professes his faith, "'Naked I came from my mother's womb, and naked I will depart. The LORD gave and the LORD has taken away; may the name of the LORD be praised.' In all this, Job did not sin by charging God with wrongdoing" (Job 1:21, 22).

However, after Satan, with God's limited permission, takes Job's health away and after his wife tells him to curse God and die (both severe tests), Job "cursed the day of his birth" (Job 3:1) for a whole chapter. Thus, he indirectly shows his angry grief over God's gift of his life and birth. It seems that even though Job is a faithful believer, human experience raises its ugly head to tempt Job to doubt God's good plan for his life.

Old age can also be a time when we give in to the temptation to let human experience replace divine experience in our rational, emotional, and/or willful lives.

Human experience usually deals with our reliance on our senses in this life, whereas divine experience looks for God's gift of endurance now in spite of our difficult circumstances and our future experiences in God's final kingdom, our goal on the road of life.

We are all at times doubting Thomases or Thomasinas. Of course, since Apostle John emphasizes in his gospel the need to have faith in Jesus as the God-man, he includes the account of Thomas' doubt about Jesus' permanent resurrection in John 20:24-29 and his profession of faith in Jesus, "My Lord and my God!" when he sees Jesus' healed wounds.

I suppose that it's easy to criticize Thomas for his doubts, but who of us has had human experience with seeing someone alive from the dead? Our human experience probably would have also clouded for us Jesus' amazing divine experience until we see and touch him.

I experienced unbelieving doubt for the first sixteen years of my life by basically thinking and living without him. However, God dispelled my doubt by convincing me that Jesus Christ fulfilled the Old Testament prophecies about him, did many mighty miracles, chose to die on the cross in my place and for my benefit, rose triumphantly from the dead, and reentered heaven to rule the universe with the Father.

How? God proved to me from his Word that Jesus is the God-man because of his followers, who expected him to kick the ruthless Romans out of Palestine and rule his people as an earthly Messiah or Ruler. Instead, his death was a crushing blow to the disciples' expectations.

However, three days after Jesus' death, his followers told people that they had seen him alive against opposition from the Jews, Romans, and Greeks and even when threatened with death. Jesus' resurrection and all of the other events, therefore, had to be historical facts because of those trustworthy eyewitnesses, whose testimonies are recorded in the Bible. Thus, I accepted Jesus as my personal Rescuer and Ruler.

Bible Discussion Questions:

1. Read Isaiah 55. In this chapter, what ways of God's thinking and acting are very different from human thoughts and ways? Explain.
2. Read Job 1-3. How do God and Satan work differently in Job's life? In ours? How do Job's faith and doubt show up in his life? How can we doubt even while we have faith? Explain.
3. Look at John 20:24-29. Put yourself in Thomas' place. How would you have reacted to the other disciples' news about seeing Jesus alive? Explain.
4. Explain in your own words the differences between God's divine experience and our human experience. Give other specific examples of that difference from the Bible.
5. How can we receive Jesus' victory to replace our human experience with his divine experience? Explain.
6. What changes in Christians' lives nowadays might have to take place for them to make that kind of spiritual progress? Explain.

* * *

One Step On Our Journey with Jesus: Confess in prayer the human-experience thinking, feeling, and deciding that still

remain in your life, and pray persistently that God's life and experience may fill your life.

* * *

Our God of grace wants us to move more and more ...

8. To new confidence in the God of the Bible:

The whole point of our Jesus journey

The point of this book is to encourage you to look and pray for God's victory in this life as you travel the hope-highway to heavenly happiness, primarily by being "bolder growin' older" in praying and witnessing. I encourage you to look forward to God's divine experience that will be fully yours as a believer beyond this life.

Don't you want to join me in the desire to become perfect in God's future, perfect universe? The purpose of this book in running a race toward that final goal through old age and death is to experience finally God's divine life fully then, while remaining human.

I illustrate God's gift of spiritual growth influencing the three areas of human experience by describing God's work in my life. First, when I was sixteen, God "talked" me into believing in him and the Bible's inspiration, largely with my God-guided reason. (See *Doubtbusters*.) Second, after I decided to leave his call to be a pastor to teach English, he allowed and used our son's death to reshape my will to send me into the ministry. Third, God dramatically healed my seven-year depression, grief, and anger at him for allowing Keith's death and other losses. (See chapter six above and *Doubtbusters*.)

I became a believer when I was sixteen years old, but God still has a lot of work to do in my life to replace my human experience with his divine experience. Old age can be a blessed time of spiritual growth as we experience God's life more and more through Jesus' victory by the Holy Spirit's power. Such spiritual progress can happen as we become "bolder growin' older" with constant prayer.

Use of the Bible in our old age

Throughout the Bible, the inspired writers describe God's thoughts, feelings, and decisions as totally opposite that of usual human experience. Thus, when we let our human thoughts, feelings, and decisions influence us in old age instead of God's Word, we doubt his divine qualities of love, goodness, grace, mercy, kindness, patience, justice, holiness, and righteousness.

Instead, we need to read and think about his Word daily. God has given me a deep and broad spiritual experience by guiding me to read through the Bible many times. I read one chapter a day so that I read it through in about three years. Then, I read through it again using a different translation. A person can also read three chapters a day to finish it in about a year. God has benefited me so that I can now relate one part of Scripture to other passages in the whole Bible. Also, he has given me insight into the relationships between the Old to New Testaments. Above all, he has caused his divine experience to overcome my human experience more and more.

I recommend using the greater amount of time we have in old age to read and apply God's Word to our lives. In that way, God will use that devotional time to replace our human-experience doubt with his divine-experience faithfulness. Also, precede each Bible reading with prayer for God's wisdom to apply his Word to your life. Afterwards, spend time in praise, thanks, confession, prayer for others, prayers for yourself, and, if necessary, laments alone with your 3-in-1 God. I find that I need to schedule my Bible reading and prayer times, or I tend to forget them.

The longer time you spend praying to the only true God of the Bible on your rocky trip, the less time you will have to doubt him in your thinking, feeling, and deciding.

Three comforting and challenging New Testament passages

For example, on a recent Sunday, our church heard a message based on Paul's five words to the young pastor in 1 Timothy 4:7b, "Train yourself to be godly." The context (1 Timothy 4:7-10) follows, "Have nothing to do with godless myths and old wives' tales; rather, train yourself to be godly. For physical training is of some value, but godliness has value for all things, holding promise for both the present life and the life to come. This is a trustworthy saying that deserves full acceptance (and for this we labor and strive), that we have put our hope in the living God, who is the Savior of all men, and especially of those who believe."

In Paul's second letter to Timothy (3:16, 17), he writes, "All Scripture is God-breathed and is useful for teaching, rebuking, correcting and training in righteousness, so that the man of God may be thoroughly equipped for every good work."

Seven observations are in order about these two passages from God's Word:

(1) Though we don't know the "myths" and "tales" to which Paul refers (1 Timothy 4:7a), we can safely assume that they are forms of human experience without God.

(2) Paul commands Timothy and us to train ourselves to be godly. The more we center our thought-life on God in prayer and our actions are done for him, the more we will banish from our minds secular thoughts not focusing on him.

(3) Notice that Paul calls us to train ourselves to focus on God. Paul's command assumes that we have not arrived at perfection yet.

(4) It's good to do arthritis exercises and other "physical training," but they are only a means to the end of honoring God as we age.

(5) Notice that God calls us to do all of our activities for him with "hope in the living God, who is the Savior of all men, and especially of those who believe."

(6) Our time on our life journey must be motivated by hope in God's final rescue of believers. His present work is to deliver believers, even though his triumph is available to all people, many of whom reject him.

(7) The solid foundation for our decreasing doubt and increasing trust in him in old age is his "God-breathed" Word, the Bible. How willing are we to let his Scriptures teach, rebuke, correct, and train us in right old-age living resulting from our deep and profound gratitude for Jesus' free gift of triumph (2 Timothy 3:16, 17)?

I go to another of many passages describing God's challenges in old age, 1 Thessalonians 5:16-18, on which I've never heard any messages except ones that I've preached, "Be joyful always, pray continually, give thanks in all circumstances, for this is God's will for you in Christ Jesus."

I'm curious why people have trouble listening to this and other passages in the New Testament. Perhaps, it's because they assume that God only commands us in the Old Testament to move toward his goals for our lives. Or maybe they think that once they believe, they need to do nothing more.

Well, they only need to read the last parts of Paul's letters to understand that God knows that once we accept Jesus as the only Path to our Father, we have a lifelong trip to our final perfection on the other side of the grave.

Bible Discussion Questions:

1. Read 1 Timothy 4:7-10. Practically, what actions can we do to train ourselves to be godly in our thinking, feeling, and doing? Explain.
2. Read 2 Timothy 3:16, 17. How do you know that Paul's description of the Bible's inspiration is true? What evidence in Scripture shows us that it is indeed God's inspired Word? (Consult *Doubtbusters! God Is My Shrink!* for answers that you can give to unbelievers near you.)
3. Read Philippians 3:10-14. What are most people's goals when they rely on human experience to guide them? What is God's goal for our old age, as we run our footrace with Paul, given in Philippians 3:10-14? Explain. How will running toward that goal as our old-age objective change how we live our lives?
4. Read 1 Thessalonians 5:16-18. How can we adopt these commands as our goals in old age? How will striving for them in the power of Jesus' victory change how we age? Explain.

* * *

One Step on Our Journey with Jesus: Ask God in persistent prayer to use the victory of Jesus' life, death, and resurrection to give you spiritual progress in accomplishing his goals for your middle and/or old age. Claim Jesus' victory for you to make you more joyful, prayerful, and thankful.

* * *

As our pace quickens on our race toward final perfection,

God wants to move us ...

Chapter Nine: *From* old losing our faith *to* new growing in our faith

9. From old "losing our faith"

Losing our faith?

Keith Drury uses the phrase "losing our faith" as follows: "For some old people, the greatest battle of faith comes at the end of life. People who die young can more easily die with a strong faith. The survivors who get old may face bigger battles. For some (especially males), the ultimate trial of faith is at the end—asking the final and ultimate question: Does God exist or has all this been a sham? This battle is usually faced silently and in the interior secret rooms of the mind. Men who are facing this battle don't even tell their wives."

First of all, I disagree with Keith that people can really "lose their faith" as they age, or anytime. In the Gospel of John, Jesus makes very clear that once people are true believers, they will always be real Christians. Just one example is necessary (John 6:35, 37, 39, 40): "Then Jesus declared, 'I am the bread of life. He who comes to me will never go hungry, and he who believes in me will never be thirsty.... All that the Father gives me will come to me, and whoever comes to me I will never drive away.... And this is the will of him who sent me, that I shall lose none of all that he has given me, but raise them up at the last day. For my Father's will is that everyone who looks to the Son and believes in him shall have eternal life, and I will raise him up at the last day."

Old-age "losing faith" is a different matter. Either the people who report such struggles never really had true faith in the first place, or they have interpreted the entrance of doubts and bitterness as "loss of faith." All genuine believers can struggle with all of the temptations in this book and maybe even fall into those sins without really losing their faith completely. However, perhaps we have been fooling ourselves all of our lives that we are Christians without really accepting the divine experience won for us by Jesus.

Having faith!

If we have only made a beginning in accepting and living the divine experience in personal relationship with the Father, Jesus, and the Holy Spirit as our one God described in the Bible, we will always have faith. None of the difficult experiences of old age can separate us from him, as inspired Paul eloquently writes in Romans 8:37-39, "No, in all these things we are more than conquerors through him who loved us. For I am convinced that neither death nor life, neither angels nor demons, neither the present nor the future, nor any powers, neither height nor depth nor anything else in all creation, will be able to separate us from the love of God that is in Christ Jesus our Lord."

Thus, our challenge in old age, as in any age, is to live as "more than conquerors," God's super-victors, through Jesus' mighty triumph. I hope that God uses this book to guide you to endure middle and old age's struggles in his strength, primarily by being "bolder growin' older"! I also hope that people will give this book to other people who might fear or struggle with old age.

The supposed "advantages" of old age

The web site www.sticksite.com has a list of tongue-in-cheek "advantages" of growing older:

> People no longer view you as a hypochondriac.
> Your supply of brain cells is down to manageable size.
> Your eyes won't get much worse.
> Adult diapers are actually kind of convenient.
> Things you buy now won't wear out.
> People won't expect you to run into a burning building or anywhere else.
> Your joints are more accurate in predicting weather than the T.V. weather forecaster.
> In a hostage situation, you are likely to be released first.
> Similarly, a reporter interviewing a 104-year-old woman asked, "And what do you think is the best thing about being 104?" She simply answered, "No peer pressure."

These humorous approaches, as with all humor, gently point out the weakness of human nature and lead us to realize that human experience can look at the positive side of life without including God.

The source of questions about God

Many older people look back at their lives and ask, "Does God really exist? How could he have been involved in my life with all of the bad things that have happened to me?" When asked how God is involved in their lives, they may reply, "I don't know." Their younger lives appear to show that they are Christians, but as they grow older and experience the aches and pain of old age, they question God's existence, though they never voice those temptations to other people.

They may also look at the news and remark to themselves, "Look at all the bad events in the world. How can God be good when he allows bad things to happen to good people?"

Such an approach by older people is, again, secular human experience apart from the Bible's divine experience. We need to repent of our human thinking, feeling, and deciding. Instead, we need to flee to God and his Word to gain his divine thoughts, emotions, and decision-making from his point-of-view.

The web site www.sticksite.com comes to our rescue with comic relief:

> My memory's not as good as it used to be; also, my memory's not as good as it used to be.
> Know how to prevent sagging? Just eat 'til the wrinkles fill out.
> I'm getting into swing dancing. Not on purpose. Some parts of my body are just prone to swinging.

It's scary when your body starts making the same noises as your coffeemaker.

These days about half of the stuff in my shopping cart says, "For fast relief."

I've tried to find a suitable exercise video for women my age, but they haven't made one titled "Buns of putty."

Don't think of it as a hot flash. Think of it as your inner child playing with matches.

Don't let old age get you down. It's too hard to get back up.

Psalm 73 describes the writer's questions about God's experience *versus* his human experience, "Surely God is good to Israel, to those who are pure in heart. But as for me, my feet had almost slipped; I had nearly lost my foothold. For I envied the arrogant when I saw the prosperity of the wicked" (verses 1-3).

Some people envy and judge rich sports and movie personalities. Indirectly, they also question God's blessings given to such celebrities, since he blesses them with a large income. The psalmist continues, "They [wicked rich people] have no struggles; their bodies are healthy and strong. They are free from the burdens common to men; they are not plagued by human ills" (verses 4 and 5).

He continues with his observation about God's blessings for wicked rich people until he questions God's comparative lack of blessings in his own life, "Surely in vain I have kept my heart pure; in vain have I have washed my hands in innocence" (verse 13). The writer wrongly contrasts the large amount of his good actions with the seeming shortage of God's blessings in his life, especially as he compares his life to rich people.

His mistake is similar to the error of Job and his "friends" when they think that some great sin brings disastrous consequences in a person's life.

In the end, God's ways are often mysterious and beyond human reasoning.

Older people can empathize with the psalmist's questioning of God because they might think, *"Look at all the good things that I did for the church, and what did they get me? Nothing, certainly not the members' gratitude!"*

The psalmist wisely keeps his questions to himself so that he will not influence other people and thus dishonor God. However, he writes, "When I tried to understand all this, it was oppressive to me till I entered the sanctuary of God; then I understood their final destiny. Surely you place them on slippery ground; you cast them down to ruin" (verses 16-18). The turning point is that the psalmist enters God's house, loses his human perspective, and gains the divine viewpoint.

He concludes, "But as for me, it is good to be near God. I have made the Sovereign LORD my refuge. I will tell of all your deeds" (verse 28). How willing are we to replace our human-centered thinking with God's thinking in his Word and to tell others about God's work in our lives?

Bible Discussion Questions:

1. What do you think about people's reports that they "have lost their faith"? What do you believe actually happened to them? Explain.

2. Read John 6:35-40. How can we reconcile Jesus' clear teachings with our experience of people's lives? Explain.

3. Read Romans 8:28-39. What comfort does this passage give you? Why? What danger might the teaching in these verses cause when people fail to believe in their human responsibility to make progress in following the true God? Explain.

4. As a corrective to such fatalism, read Romans 12-14. How do these chapters correct the thinking that we only have to believe in but not obey God? Explain.

5. Read Psalm 73. How can we find a similar change in perspective from our human experience to God's outlook? Explain. How can we gain the courage and the words to share our testimonies about God's work in our lives the way the psalmist resolves at the psalm's very end? Explain.

* * *

One Step on Our Journey with Jesus: If you have questions about God's involvement in your life and the universe, confess that you have let your human experience color your thinking. Ask God to give you his perspective through his Word and other Christians.

*   *   *

As we race toward God's great goal, he moves us ...

9. To new growing in our faith

Psalm 73 describes how we can grow in our faith. The key is changing our perspective from reliance on our human experience to depending on God's point-of-view. In other words, we need to take God's larger view of life. For example, some people pray fervently for God's healing from cancer in a loved one's life. However, that person dies instead. Such deep disappointment can color our lives.

What we fail to take into account is that our loved one's death starts that person's healing, if he or she is a Christian. The truth is that we may not have been ready to let our loved one go. Our motivation for prayer may be selfish, and God will not honor selfish prayers. Also, he answers our prayers his way, not ours. After all, he's God and we're not.

However, how do we grow in our faith? I've heard people say that when we believe, we don't need to grow in faith. They would have us believe that we are no longer sinners. They claim that sin may be in us, but we no longer sin.

The commandments in the Book of Hebrews

If we are no longer sinners, why would God guide the New Testament writers to give us so many commandments? Yes, commandments are not just limited to the Old Testament, but are also in the last parts of the letters and throughout the gospels. For example, the writer to the Hebrews gives us thirty-six calls to obedience in chapters twelve and thirteen:

"Let us throw off everything that hinders..." (12:1).

"Let us run with perseverance the race marked out for us..." (12:1).

"Let us fix our eyes on Jesus, the author and perfecter of our faith..." (12:2).

"Consider him who endured such opposition from sinful men, so that you will not grow weary and lose heart..." (12:3).

"Do not make light of the Lord's discipline and do not lose heart when he rebukes you..." (12:5).

"Endure hardship as discipline..." (12:7).

"Strengthen your feeble arms and weak knees. Make level paths for your feet..." (12:12, 13).

"Make every effort to live in peace with all men and to be holy..." (12:14).

"See to it that no one misses the grace of God and that no bitter root grows up..." (12:15).

"See that no one is sexually immoral, or is godless..." (12:16).

"See to it that you do not refuse him who speaks..." (12:25).

"Let us be thankful, and so worship God acceptably with reverence and awe..." (12:28)

"Keep on loving each other as brothers..." (13:1).

"Remember those in prison as if you were their fellow prisoners, and those who are mistreated as if you yourselves were suffering" (13:3).

"Marriage should be honored by all, and the marriage bed kept pure..." (13:4).

"Keep your lives free from the love of money and be content with what you have..." (13:5).

"Remember your leaders who spoke the word of God to you..." (13:7).

"Consider the outcome of [your leaders'] way of life and imitate their faith" (13:7).

"Do not be carried away by all kinds of strange teachings" (13:9).

"Let us, then, go to [Jesus, our high priest, who was crucified outside the city, the same way the sacrificial animals' bodies were burned] outside the camp, bearing the disgrace he bore" (13:13).

"Through Jesus, therefore, let us continually offer to God a sacrifice of praise..." (13:15).

"And do not forget to do good and to share with others..." (13:16).

"Obey your leaders and submit to their authority" (13:17).

"Obey them so that their work will be a joy, not a burden..." (13:17).

"Pray for us" (12:18).

I call this list God's Thirty-Six New Commandments by the writer to the Hebrews. These new-covenant goals follow the writer's demonstration in the first eleven chapters of Jesus' deity and humanity given in his life and death for God's forgiveness.

Thus, just as God's brief description of his release of Israel from slavery in Egypt (Exodus 20:2) precedes the Ten Commandments, so the writer expounds in the first eleven chapters Jesus' release of us and Old Testament saints (chapter 11) from our slavery to sin and Satan. These new-covenant commandments in relationship with Jesus, our only High Priest, present us with our goals for holy living that involve our whole lives guided by the Holy Spirit. They also provide us with the directions for our words and actions as we use his divine power.

My point is that God gives us commands because we haven't arrived at perfection yet. We're still sinners. God our Judge's verdict of "guilty" is gone because of Jesus' victory, but we still struggle to overcome the sins within us with the power of his deliverance on our path toward our final goal. Therefore, we need to have stronger and stronger faith to be more and more effective as his agents.

Bruce Leiter

God's glorification when we believe

Furthermore, the passage Romans 8:29, 30 describes God's five actions when we first trust in Jesus as the Way to our Father. Romans 8:30c shows the last two divine actions, "Those he justified, he also glorified." When God declares us "not guilty" and right with him ("justified" us), he also glorifies us. What does that glorification involve?

Paul also helps us understand how God glorifies us when we first believe in him. In Second Corinthians chapter three, he contrasts the old and new situations of God's covenant with Abraham and with us. In verse six, he writes, "He has made us competent as ministers of a new covenant—not of the letter but of the Spirit; for the letter kills, but the Spirit gives life."

The "letter" is the outward form of the old covenant's commandments as Israel's national law. However, the Holy Spirit works in us to increase our loving inner and outer obedience to our loving Boss Jesus.

Paul continues in chapter six to contrast the fading brightness or glory of the old, national covenant symbolized by God's brightness on Moses' face. He uses a veil to hide that glory when he leaves God's presence. Here, Paul contrasts that fading glory with the steadily increasing brightness of God's glory in our lives, "But whenever anyone turns to the Lord, the veil is taken away. Now the Lord is the Spirit, and wherever the Spirit of the Lord is, there is freedom. And we, who with unveiled faces, all reflect the Lord's glory, are being transformed into his likeness with ever-increasing glory, which comes from the Lord, who is the Spirit" (2 Corinthians 3:16-18).

Several thoughts come to mind about Paul's writing here:

(1) In Exodus 34:29-35, Moses puts on a veil because his face shines with God's brightness or glory after he talks with God until that glory fades. Paul compares that piece of cloth with the unbelief of God's people in his day rejecting God's brightness.

(2) Has God removed the unbelief veil in your life? If so, he has also put a "spark" of his power or glory in your heart, which is the figurative place in your life that thinks, feels, and decides.

(3) According to Paul, the Holy Spirit from the Father through Jesus gives us freedom from having to follow God's many commandments in order to receive his rescue, according to the people's distortion of the national form of the old covenant. He frees us from Satan's domination to follow Jesus' loving guidance with our responding love.

(4) However, God begins the transforming process to become more and more like him "with ever-increasing glory" (verse 18—literally "glory to glory"), the way he creates Adam and Eve in the first place.

(5) We need to praise our 3-in-1 God that he enables us to grow in his glory with his transforming power because of Jesus' amazing victory.

(6) Such progress does not happen overnight. It also involves our human responsibility to run the race in the strength of Jesus' triumph, as all of God's commands show.

Why we run the race toward God's final destination

Furthermore, some people assume that when they retire from their regular occupation, they also retire from running the race that Paul describes in Philippians 3:10-14: "I want to know Christ and the power of his resurrection and the fellowship of sharing in his suffering, becoming like him in his death, and so, somehow, to attain to the resurrection from the dead. Not that I already have obtained all of this or have already been made perfect, but I press on to take hold of that for which Christ Jesus took hold of me. Brothers, I do not consider myself yet to have taken hold of it. But one thing I do: Forgetting what is behind and straining toward what is ahead, I press on toward the goal to win the prize for which God has called me heavenward in Christ Jesus."

(1) Paul and we in old age have God's great goal to know Christ. Of course, we who have given our lives to Jesus already know him in love personally, but we seek to know him more and more fully as we pass through middle into old age.

(2) We also need to accept and know the fellowship of sharing in his suffering. We will all suffer old-age changes and losses, but Jesus suffered for us incredibly more than we ever will. When we suffer in old age, Jesus went through much greater suffering in order to support

us through our constant prayers to move toward his future gift of final perfection, as Paul also writes.

(3) We with Paul also need to know the power of his resurrection in greater measure. We believers participate in his suffering, death, and resurrection throughout our lives. Thus, we can base part of our prayers on claiming Jesus' suffering and death so that God will overcome our lives' sinful tendencies and other evil influences on us. We also need to claim Jesus' resurrection to replace our old-nature characteristics with God's gift of new-nature qualities like the fruit of the Holy Spirit in Galatians 5:22, 23.

(4) Paul gives us God's great goal for our present lives in verse 11, the resurrection from the dead (literally, "from corpses"). Even though we won't obtain God's goal until he raises us from the grave, Paul nonetheless leads us to make our present goal in life our final resurrection perfection, even though we won't gain it this side of death.

(5) Paul makes that last detail very clear in verse 12. If Paul states clearly that he is not perfect yet, I certainly cannot claim to be perfect. However, Jesus' perfect life and death provide God's pronouncement of "not guilty" in my life so that he, as my Judge, **considers** me perfect because of Jesus' perfection. However, like Paul, my daily life is far from perfect. That contrast is the "already-not-yet" of the good news. My just Judge, God, "already" declares and considers me perfect

because of Jesus' perfection, but my life is "not yet" even close to being flawless.

(6) The terms "press on" and "straining" that Paul uses to describe his great effort to run Jesus' journey come from the Olympic races. Similar to the Olympic runners' goal of winning their races, we are in a race to win the prize of resurrection perfection. The finish line is the end of this existence. However, the prize is not a wreath but our final, flawless bliss in the new creation after Jesus returns.

(7) Our incentive for persevering in running that race, which all believers will win in Jesus' powerful strength, is the future new creation. At that time, as God's voice in Revelation 21:3, 4 announces, "Now the dwelling of God is with men, and he will live with them. They will be his people, and God himself will be with them and be their God. He will wipe away every tear from their eyes. There will be no more death or mourning or crying or pain, for the old order of things has passed away." Such a firm basis for our hope should inspire and motivate us to go through all the suffering and losses of old age.

In my conclusion of chapter nine, I want to share with you my prayers, from which you can get some guidance in praying. I found that when I didn't structure my prayers, my mind would tend to wander to other thoughts. As a result, the following prayer summarizes what I pray with my mind as I swim laps at the pool for half an hour:

1. I praise God for his creative and providential power in making and maintaining his universe.
2. I praise God for his saving and sanctifying power in rescuing and restoring all believers.
3. I praise him for Jesus' humiliation (birth, life, and death) and his exaltation (resurrection, return to heaven, and ruling the universe with the Father).
4. I pray that God will use the power that Jesus released when he humiliated (humbled) himself for my deliverance to overcome all three of the evil influences in all believers' lives: their sinful natures, the devil and the demons' attacks and influence, and the tempting world in all believers' lives.
5. I pray that God will use the power of Jesus' exaltation to replace more and more our old-nature qualities with the new-nature qualities that he has given all believers. Then, I ask for God's progress on specific ones in my life, for example, for patience to replace my impatience, and self-control to replace my impulsiveness.
6. I pray that God's Word will spread through believers' witnessing and their lives throughout the world so that Jesus will come soon. I also pray for Jesus' victory in the lives of all the people on my prayer list.

7. Finally, I pray for God's blessing on my retirement, especially my writing career, by strengthening many people spiritually through the books that he guides me to write.

Bible Discussion Questions:

1. Read Hebrews 12 and 13. How can we put these thirty-six commandments into practice? Explain. (I suggest that you pray that God will enable you to put into practice three of them each week for twelve weeks.)

2. Read Romans 8:29, 30 and 2 Corinthians 3:16-18. What is God's glory? What evidence should Christians see in themselves of God's gift of glory? What can we do to grow in God's glory? Explain.

3. Read Exodus 34:29-35. What does this passage tell you about God, Israel, and Moses? Explain.

4. Read Philippians 3:10-14. How much desire do present-day Christians have to run the race toward our future, perfect inheritance? Explain. How can we run toward our final perfection as Jesus' free gift of grace? Explain.

5. In your own words, what does this book's title mean for your life? Share with the group all of the ways you can be "bolder growin' older."

* * *

One Step on Our Journey with Jesus: Challenge yourself to read, meditate on, and/or memorize three of the Hebrews 12 and 13 commandments every week for twelve weeks. Pray daily for Jesus' triumph to give you his Holy Spirit to put them into practice. Reread this book at some point for insights into God's Word that you missed the first time, and pray to God for his strength to follow Jesus more and more.

* * *

As we speed up our paces with Jesus toward his new universe,

God moves us ...

Chapter Ten: *From* morbid fixation on death *to* hopeful assurance about life beyond death

10. From old morbid fixation on death:

Many older folks focus on death and grief

Keith Drury writes that according to his interviews with older folks, many of them are stuck focusing on death, "Older people face death frequently." Somewhere in their fifties, many of them begin to read the obituaries and keep track of the number of people older than they are who have died. As they age, they see that number dwindling.

My dad said that he read the obits to see if he was there. When he wasn't, he was happy. God saved him at the age of seventy-seven!

Keith observes that older people bury parents, then friends and spouses. At those funerals because younger pastors don't know what to say about hope beyond the grave, they focus on the loved one's life, as if all that counts is what people do. Our culture bombards us with the message that all that matters is living a full life. He goes on, "This is how the aged plunge into an ever-spiraling funk of morbidity thinking only of their coming departure and thinking little of the life beyond. Morbidity is a besetting temptation of old age."

A plaque in a newspaper department store ad says, "LIFE IS ABOUT THE JOURNEY, NOT THE DESTINATION." It seems to me that many people nowadays are living out that slogan. However, when they face death as often as many older people do, I can see why they get morbid and discouraged. The Bible's Good News says that life is about *both* the journey *and* the destination! It is that truth in the Bible that prompts us to go on our trip toward an amazing future.

A webpage at www.cigna.com has some helpful observations about grieving old people: "Older people express their grief the same ways as younger and middle-age adults, but because of their age and other life experiences, older adults may:

- Experience several losses in a short period of time. Such stressful circumstances may cause them to feel overwhelmed, numb, or have a hard time expressing their grief.
- Not be aware that they are grieving. Older adults experience losses related to aging…. They may feel sad and experience other signs of grieving without knowing that they are grieving.
- Be unwilling to tell other people that they are grieving.
- Have long-term illnesses, including mental and physical disabilities, that interfere with their ability to grieve.

- Lack the support system that they had in the past.... These older adults may feel lonely and think that they have no one to confide in."

Thus, it's no wonder that a number of senior citizens get stuck thinking about death because they have never really resolved their grief about all of the losses in their lives.

The cigna.com article goes on, "Some older adults may develop unresolved guilt or complications associated with grieving. This may occur more often in older adults because they are more likely to experience:

- Many losses in a short period of time.
- The death of their friends, including their spouses. Older adults who lose their spouses may suffer many losses, including their best friends, and their social contacts.
- Losses that occur as part of the natural aging process, such as loss of beauty and physical strength.
- Loss of their independence or the development of illness or other conditions that are common in older adults.
- Anticipation of losing someone or something special to them."

A desperate, dark psalm

The writer of Psalm 88 reflects the darkness of depression and some older folks' dwelling morbidly on death as follows: "O LORD, the God who saves me, day and night I cry out before you. May my prayer come before you; turn your ear to my cry. For my soul is full of trouble and my life draws near the grave. I am counted among those who go down to the pit; I am like a man without strength. I am set apart with the dead, like the slain who lie in the grave, whom you remember no more, who are cut off from your care" (verses 1-5). Note the writer's depressed despair and desperation that are similar to many older people's feelings.

However, the question arises, why would God guide people to include this psalm in his inspired Word? In response, I point out the psalmist's focus on his God and his honest expression of his feelings. Those features make this psalm a model for our prayers anytime we experience severe losses, especially in old age.

The writer continues, "You have put me in the lowest pit, in the darkest depths. Your wrath lies heavily upon me; you overwhelmed me with all your waves. You have taken me from my closest friends and have made me repulsive to them. I am confined and cannot escape; my eyes are dim with grief. I call to you, O LORD, every day; I spread out my hands to you" (verses 6-9). What is positive about this psalm? Very little. However, the psalmist expresses his grief, and I have found that when I express my grief openly and prayerfully focus on God, he comes close to me and eventually comforts me.

However, a lot of people shy away from praying about their losses because thinking about them causes emotional pain. The key to receiving God's peace and comfort is to face and express your emotions instead of escaping them or bottling them up inside of you.

Then, the psalmist desperately cries out to God for his rescue, "I cry out to you for help, O LORD; in the morning my prayer comes before you.... You have taken my companions and loved ones from me; the darkness is my closest friend" (verses 13, 18). He doesn't experience God's rescue in this dark psalm but implores God to deliver him from his losses and his dark despair. Such desperate pleas and clinging to God provide the only hope. As a result, the glimmer of hope is that he focuses on the God who delivers us now and perfectly in our next life.

The Ecclesiastes writer's "meaninglessness"

Another passage that has been questioned as to whether it should be in the Bible is the Book of Ecclesiastes. It begins as follows: "The words of the Teacher, son of David, king in Jerusalem: 'Meaningless! Meaningless!' says the Teacher, 'Utterly meaningless! Everything is meaningless! What does a man gain from all his labor at which he toils under the sun'" (1:1-3)? To understand the Teacher's exclamations, though, notice that he uses the phrase "under the sun." When he uses this phrase in this book, the Teacher describes life lived apart from God that is, therefore, meaningless. The Hebrew word for "meaningless" pictures the emptiness of a puff of breath that disappears quickly. Therefore, the Teacher uses a jarring metaphor about the total emptiness of a life that ignores or rejects the true God of the Bible.

The Teacher, probably Solomon, experiences many different life events to observe that life is meaningless without God. In the last chapter he commands the younger generation, "Remember your Creator in the days of your youth, before the days of trouble come and the years approach when you will say, 'I find no pleasure in them'—before the moon and the stars grow dark and the clouds return after the rain…" (12:1, 2).

The word "remember" means not just a mental ability but also acting on that memory. In other words, he advises young people to believe in and obey their Creator while they anticipate the Creator's joining the human race in Jesus Christ.

Furthermore, the writer continues the chapter by comparing old age with a ramshackle house. For example, he says that old age is a time "when the keepers of the house tremble, and the strong men stoop, when the grinders [teeth] cease because they are few, and those looking through the windows [eyes] grow dim … when men are afraid of heights and of dangers in the streets … and the grasshopper drags himself along and desire no longer is stirred. Then man goes to his eternal home and mourners go about in the streets" (12:3-5). This description is a general observation to which people who focus their lives on God are exceptions.

However, many older people feel as if their lives are meaningless if they aren't focused on God. Thus, it's important to call our younger people to follow Jesus before their lives fall into the despair of old age.

Bible Discussion Questions:

1. Read Psalm 88. Why do you think God included this psalm in the Bible? What is its value for your life? How can it change your prayer life? Explain.
2. Most other psalms have a positive ending. Why do you think that this psalm is dark throughout? Where do you think is the psalmist's hope? Explain. What is our hope in old age?
3. Read Ecclesiastes 1 and 12. Why do people feel uncomfortable with the writer's message about life without God? How do you feel about his advice in chapter twelve? Explain.

* * *

One Step on Our Journey with Jesus: Recall people's unloving actions and your life's losses. "Be bolder growin' older" by praying privately laments like Psalms 39 and 88. Persistently tell God honestly and openly with tears the anger and/or anxiety that you feel about those events in your life. At the same time, persistently confess your selfishness in wanting your own loss-free plan for your life rather than God's plan allowing those losses for your good.

* * *

As we near our final goal, resurrection perfection,
God wants to move us ...

10. <u>To new hopeful assurance of life beyond death:</u>

I have already described how God can use older folks as volunteers and in other activities, but how can we be assured about life beyond the grave to make our approach to death meaningful?

Our new bodies replacing these old, weak bodies

Moreover, what will our resurrection bodies be like as one beautiful facet of God's salvation diamond? Not much is written in the Old Testament about the future resurrection except a few hints and Daniel 12:1-3, a passage describing a time during and after God's defeat of evil political leaders, "At that time Michael, the great prince who protects your people, will arise. There will be a time of distress such as has not happened from the beginning of nations until then. But at that time your people—everyone whose name is written in the book—will be delivered. Multitudes who sleep in the dust of the earth will awake: some to everlasting life, others to shame and everlasting contempt. Those who are wise will shine like the brightness of the heavens, and those who lead many to righteousness, like the stars for ever and ever."

During this meaningful part of our increasingly rapid cruise toward our final triumph, we notice that the angel in Daniel's vision describes a great heightening of human trouble and struggle before the general resurrection of all people's bodies. The same division between two groups of people takes place in Jesus' symbolic description of the sheep and the goats in Matthew 25.

We also note that believers' bodies will shine with God's glittering glory. That description is another way of saying that our bodies will shine like our sun, which is a star. However, we will have new eyes that will be able to see our bright glare without squinting.

Moreover, Paul expands on the teaching in the Book of Daniel with his message from God in Philippians 3:20, 21. Compared to unbelievers, who only have an earthly citizenship, "our citizenship is in heaven. And we eagerly await a Savior from there, the Lord Jesus Christ, who, by the power that enables him to bring everything under his control, will transform our lowly bodies so that they will be like his glorious body." Notice that Jesus will bring our citizenship from heaven to us when he comes the second time.

Then, believers' bodies will shine with the dazzling power of God, as the angel told Daniel. They will also have bodies like Jesus' body, which was the same physical body with his scars from the crucifixion nails and with which he ate broiled fish in their presence.

Also, with that body, he could enter a room instantly, even though the doors were locked. We true believers will have our own kind of Transportation something like Ezekiel's, Elijah's, Philip's, and John's occasional way to get around, the Holy Spirit. However, our

Mode of Transportation will be permanent like Jesus' ability to go through locked doors.

An amazing description of our resurrected bodies

One final passage shows conclusively that our risen bodies will be these same bodies perfected with resurrection power. God enables Paul to describe our risen bodies in First Corinthians chapter fifteen, where Paul makes the case for Jesus' resurrection. He then writes that believers, too, will experience the resurrection of their bodies because of that historical event.

The believers at Corinth had difficulty believing that teaching, because the Greeks believed that the body was completely evil and that when they died, their souls would permanently escape their corrupt bodies.

On the other hand, the Bible clearly teaches that God creates Adam and Eve's bodies perfect but that evil is a foreign invader to be repelled some day when we die, if we trust in the Messiah, Jesus, as the Path to the future new creation. Therefore, Paul goes to great lengths to clarify God's future provision of the resurrection body.

In 1 Corinthians 15:20-23, Paul asserts, "But Christ has indeed been raised from the dead, the firstfruits of those who have fallen asleep. For since death came through a man [Adam], the resurrection of the dead came through a man [Jesus]." For Paul, Adam is the representative head of the whole human race, while Jesus is the representative head of all believers as his body. "For as in Adam all die, so in Christ all [believers] will be made alive." I insert "believers" because of the next verse, "But each in his own turn: Christ, the firstfruits; then, when he comes, those who belong to him." This verse teaches that Christ's rising from death will lead to the bodily resurrection of all true believers.

However, what will our risen bodies be like? We already know that they will be like Jesus' body. Paul in verses 37-41 writes that our future bodies will be different from our present ones just as different creatures and stars have different characteristics. Then, he compares our present, fallen bodies to seeds planted in the ground. The same seed grows into a plant, but it is not completely different. "So will it be with the resurrection of the dead. The body that is sown is perishable, it is raised imperishable; it is sown in dishonor, it is raised in glory; it is sown in weakness, it is raised in power; it is sown a natural body, it is raised a spiritual body."

Notice that our present fallen body and the risen one will be both similar and different. The new body won't wear out ("imperishable"). It will also be glorious (light-bright), powerful, and spiritual (filled and completely controlled by the Holy Spirit).

On the other hand, our risen bodies, like seeds planted in the ground, will be our fallen, weak bodies. When Jesus returns, however, God renews them by grace and makes them grow like a harvest of perfect bodies. The same seed that is planted like our dead bodies will be raised as an eternal "plant" that will never wear out.

What a great hope we have for perfect bodies as we run toward our goal with these "growin'-older tents"! If we cling to this biblical truth, we have no reason to get morbid and discouraged as we face death.

In 1 Corinthians 15:50, Paul gives us another clue to understand our new bodies, "I declare to you, brothers, that flesh and blood cannot inherit the kingdom of God, nor does the perishable inherit the imperishable." These weak bodies have "flesh and blood," but our future bodies will not have "flesh and blood," though Paul doesn't explain his statement. However, he, instead, breaks out into praise, "But thanks be to God! He gives us the victory through our Lord Jesus Christ" (verse 57).

Paul also drives home in Philippians 3:20, 21 his point that Jesus will change our present "tents" into our fully-perfected resurrection bodies: "But our citizenship is in heaven. And we eagerly await a Savior from there, the Lord Jesus Christ, who, by the power that enables him to bring everything under his control, will transform our lowly bodies so that they will be like his glorious body." We are citizens of heaven, God's throne room; but Jesus, when he returns, will make our fallen, weak, frail bodies into amazing, perfect bodies like his. Come soon, Jesus!

Bible Discussion Questions:

1. Read Daniel 12:1-3. What comforts you about God's teaching in these verses? What is uncomfortable about them? Explain.
2. Read Philippians 3:20, 21. How does the fact that our future bodies will be like Jesus' resurrected body make you feel? Explain.
3. Read 1 Corinthians 15. What ideas jump out at you about Jesus' resurrection and our future resurrection? Explain.
4. On a scale of 1 to 10 with 10 the highest, how much do you want Jesus to come back to resurrect believers? Why?

* * *

One Step on Our Journey with Jesus: Fill your mind with praise for the hope of our final resurrection and our future entrance in the new, perfected universe.

Our future, heavenly singleness

In the beginning, the LORD made Eve out of Adam's body to become his suitable helper. The goal of every Christian marriage is unity and equality in status under God, because both spouses are made fully in God's likeness (Genesis 1:26, 27).

However, God also gave males and females different roles within that relationship: Adam as the servant-leader serving Eve's needs, and Eve supporting and submitting to Adam's servant-leadership, not his dominance. In our fallen state, those functions are our immediate travel goals, as Paul lays them out in Ephesians 5:22-33, if we are married.

If God calls us to have his gift of singleness, as he inspires Paul to describe in First Corinthians chapter seven, we give our lives to serve him single-mindedly. Interestingly, it's perhaps hard for us to imagine, but Jesus' description of the resurrection is that there will be no marriage in our future state (Mark 12:18-27).

Such teaching challenges our thinking. Apparently, we'll all be single like the angels in the new creation. Our sole attention will focus on pleasing our 3-in-1 Lord. Likewise, Jesus teaches that there is a spiritual gift of singleness (Matthew 19:10-12) in a culture where almost everyone is married.

If you are single on your trip toward God's goal, you are not alone and need not be lonely. The three-Persons-in-one God can be with you as you run that road. In addition, other Christians are ready to tread that treacherous trail with you in a God-honoring, Bible-preaching-and-teaching church, if you aren't already involved in one.

Our future family relationships renewed

That comment leads us into an examination of another relationship to be renewed. Someone once said, "Everything is relatives," as a variation on the false saying "Everything is relative." How will our family relationships change?

Jesus gives us a little peek at our future when his mother and brothers travel from Nazareth to Capernaum, Jesus' ministry "headquarters," "to take charge" of Jesus (literally, to arrest him), because "they said, 'He is out of his mind'" (Mark 3:21). When they arrive at the preaching place, they send for him.

Jesus' response may startle us, "Who are my mother and brothers?" he asks. Then he looks at those seated in a circle around him and says, "Here are my mother and brothers! Whoever does God's will is my brother and sister and mother" (Mark 3:31-35). We who are in a family-oriented culture might think that Jesus is unnecessarily harsh.

However, Jesus' choice is between obeying his family's desires that he follow *their* path or submitting to God the Father's road toward the cross. People so often take it for granted that their families know best. On the other hand, when and if our relatives' will conflicts with God's direction for our lives or his inspired Bible, we must follow our covenant God's ways, while at the same time respecting our family's ideas.

The commandment to honor our father and our mother does not always mean that we obey them, especially when we get out on our own. God may have a different direction for our lives from our family's wishes.

The conclusion that we can draw is that we will no longer be in extended families or clans in the new creation. Rather, all believers will be one, huge, perfect family as God's adopted children and as Jesus' adopted siblings.

Bible Discussion Questions:

1. Why do you think some people assume that single people should get married?
2. Read 1 Corinthians 6:12-20. What principles about sex does God give us? How should we approach the desire to go to bed with someone to whom we're attracted? Explain.
3. What other biblical stories and teachings call us to keep sex within marriage?
4. What do you think about the charge that people are old-fashioned if they don't have sex until marriage? What does the Bible say about our culture's approaches to singleness and marriage?
5. Read Mark 3:21, 31-35. What is your reaction to Jesus' response to his family's words and actions when they arrive and summon him? What lesson can we draw from Jesus' words? Explain.

* * *

One Step on Our Journey with Jesus: Ask God for his gifts of courage and words to enable you to repair any broken relationships with family members or other people from whom you are estranged. Ask God also to strengthen your relationship with him so that it's the most important covenant relationship in your life. Then, seek to be God's agent of blessing to the people around you.

* * *

After God's comforting teachings about our resurrection bodies and relationships, we examine Jesus' final vision to John in Revelation 20-22, where we discover our final goal of God's resurrection destination. In chapter 20, Satan is released at the end of the 1,000 years and gathers his troops to battle God's people. When God's fire of judgment makes short work of their rebellion, they end up in the lake of burning sulfur just the way the earlier beasts did (20:7-10). I believe that the repetition of the two battles in chapters 19 and 20 points to only one battle described in two ways, while the second one adds more details.

The same kind of repetition happens in Genesis chapters one and two, where the second creation account provides more details about God's creative work. In Revelation, Jesus, in his visions given to the Apostle John, does a lot of this same kind of repetition concerning the time between Jesus' two comings, while progressively giving more details about Jesus' Second Coming in each vision.

According to my interpretation of Revelation 20, at the end of this present age, the figurative period of time called the "thousand years," when Satan has been hindered from preventing the spread of the gospel to all nations, the devil will be released from captivity. Given present-day events, I believe that that release has perhaps already happened or might happen soon.

Then, after the devil's defeat and the general resurrection, God will judge all people during the Final Judgment. Relevant for our long journey toward the new creation is the observation, "Then death and Hades were thrown into the lake of fire. The lake of fire is the second death" (Revelation 20:14).

Death will die. What a comfort God's Word is for those of us who fear death! Thus, we celebrate our trip toward the new heaven and new earth revealed in Revelation 21.

The future "rapture" of believers giving us hope

Where will we believers be when Jesus remakes our present home into our future, perfect residence?

We must approach the following Bible reference with no preconceptions. Many people assume that Jesus will come invisibly to snatch away living believers to heaven. Therefore, they go to 1

Thessalonians 4:13-18 with that idea. However, let's approach God's Word without any prior ideas.

In that passage, Paul writes to the believers in Thessalonica to overcome their fears about their loved ones who have died since Paul's preaching about Jesus' Second Coming. Their fear is that the believing people who have died will lose out on that future event.

Paul's pastoral response is, "Brothers, we do not want you to be ignorant about those who fall asleep [die], or to grieve like the rest of men, who have no hope." Notice that he does not say that we aren't supposed to grieve our loved ones' deaths, but that such grief should be mixed with hope about the future.

Then, he clearly describes the event in which believers will participate and for which they should hope. God will bring with Jesus the souls of those who have already died when he returns (verse 14a).

Will his coming be silent and invisible? This passage doesn't come close to saying so. "For the Lord himself will come down from heaven, with a loud command, with the voice of the archangel and with the trumpet call of God, and the dead in Christ will rise first" (verse 16). If we are still alive when Jesus comes back, he will bring back with him the souls of our beloved believers who have died so they can enter their resurrected bodies.

Then, "after that, we who are still alive and are left will be caught up [the Latin version's meaning is "raptured"] together with them in the clouds to meet the Lord in the air" (verses 16, 17). The resurrection bodies of all believers, united with their souls, will break the law of gravity and rise to have a great reunion in the atmosphere with each other and Jesus. However, the saying "what goes up must come down" applies here, too. The Greek word translated "meet" has a technical meaning for the actions of a delegation of a town's citizens that go out to welcome ("meet") a government dignitary and usher him back to their town, when he comes to visit.

As Jesus descends, he will fulfill the angels' prediction in Acts 1:11, "This same Jesus, who has been taken from you into heaven, will come back in the same way you have seen him go into heaven." We who are still alive in our new, perfect bodies will then meet him and all other believers in the sky.

The usual, technical meaning for the word "meet" *seems* to conflict with Jesus' teaching in John 14:1-3 after he announces his departure, "Do not let your hearts be troubled. Trust in God; trust also in me. In my Father's house are many rooms; if it were not so, I would have told you. I am going there to prepare a place for you. And if I go and prepare a place for you, I will come back and take you to be with me that you may be where I am."

However, if Jesus comes back to us, isn't he then going take us to heaven? All Jesus says in John 14 is that he will take us to be with him in God the Father's heavenly palace.

Similarly, the 1 Thessalonians chapter four passage doesn't specifically say where our final destination will be. It may be heaven, but other passages like Acts 1:11 seem to point elsewhere, because the angel announces to the apostles that Jesus will return in the same way he left.

God's purifying of the earth

Let's go a step further as we near the end of our tremendous trip by hanging a little longer in the sky. What will happen next? In 2 Peter 3:10-13, we have Peter's clue to the next event on our journey, after he answers doubters about Jesus' Second Coming: "But the day of the Lord will come like a thief. The heavens will disappear with a roar, the elements will be destroyed by fire, and the earth and everything in it will be laid bare. Since everything will be destroyed in this way, what kind of people ought you to be? You ought to live holy and godly lives as you look forward to the day of God and speed its coming. That day will bring about the destruction of the heavens by fire, and the elements will melt in the heat. But in keeping with his promise we are looking forward to a new heaven and a new earth, the home of righteousness." I believe that this unexpected turn of events will happen when we are suspended in the atmosphere, as the 1 Thessalonians chapter four passage describes during our wait for God's creation of a new universe.

Thus, God's fire of judgment, like Sodom and Gomorrah's destruction, will cleanse the old, sinful heaven and earth to make way for the same universe to be renewed without any effects of sin. If the new heaven and earth will be the home of righteousness (verse 13), where the inhabitants will be perfect, how can we go up to meet Jesus and flit off to heaven? In that case, no righteous inhabitants will inhabit that new cosmos.

Furthermore, notice that the fire will burn this present heaven and earth. Then, God will remake this universe into a perfect one. The reason that I make that observation is that the Greek word translated "new" in "new earth" is the word meaning "new and improved," not "brand-new."

On our path toward our goal of permanent, powerful perfection, such comforting teaching should motivate us, as Peter wrote, "to live holy and godly lives as you look forward to the day of God and speed its coming" (2 Peter 3:11b, 12a). In other words, God's teaching about Jesus' return gives us a reason to focus our lives more and more on him rather than on acquiring the things of this life that will be burned up.

It also makes us want to share the good news about the 3-in-1 God of the Bible and Jesus' victory in order to "speed" Jesus' coming. Of course, God has already planned the time of Jesus' return, but our loving testimonies will seem to hurry up that event from a human viewpoint. Thus, God wants to rescue people through us, his agents who are very weak in our own strength but strong in his power.

Paul's command in 1 Corinthians 10:31 must be our goal, "So whether you eat or drink or whatever you do, do it all for the glory of God." Paul's inspired guideline is a good one to guide our lives as we face growing older, dying, and eventually meeting Jesus in the air.

Why? God will burn and purify this old earth from the effects of human selfism.

Bible Discussion Questions:

1. Read Revelation 20:1-10. If the 1,000-year period describes the present time between Jesus' first and second comings, the end of chapter 19 describes in a figurative way Jesus' second coming as he returns triumphantly on a white horse, and then chapter 20 starts over with his first coming at the beginning of the figurative millennium. If this understanding is correct, what is your reaction to this passage?

    On the other hand, if the period of 1,000 years is a literal future time, how do you feel about Revelation 20:1-10?

    Regardless of the correct interpretation, how will God change your life and your prayers as you live with the hope that these verses give you? How much of a real difference does it make whether the 1,000 years are future or present? Why?

2. Read 1 Thessalonians 4:13-18. What hope, comfort, and challenge do these verses give you? Explain.

3. Read 2 Peter chapter three. What are your reactions to God's fiery future for the universe described in verses 7, 10, 12b, 13? How does Peter's description compare to God's miraculous rescue of Shadrach, Meshach, and Abednego in Daniel chapter three? To God's judgment of Sodom and Gomorrah (Genesis 19)? Explain.

4. What is Peter's conclusion about how our lives should change in verses 11 and 12a? Put in your own words how God will use these three passages to improve your life.

* * *

One Step on Our Journey with Jesus: Thank the Lord in your prayers that our future as believers is secure because of Jesus' life, death, and resurrection. Express your gratitude in your daily life for the tangible hope that he has given you.

* * *

Jesus' Final Judgment of all humans

We'll have to hang in the air a little longer on the last leg of our journey, while we discover the Final Judgment. Matthew 25:31-46 is Jesus' figurative description of that final event. Of course, you know that all people, raised from the dead, will come before his throne of judgment. God is clearly just in punishing people's imperfections. The emphasis in the symbolic judgment of the sheep on Jesus' right hand and the goats on his left is what they did or didn't do for Jesus, who came to them during their lives in the guise of people in need.

However, the sheep will not in any way earn Jesus' verdict of "not guilty" or his gift of eternal life. The key verse for our understanding is verse 34, "Then the King will say to those on his right, 'Come, you who are blessed by my Father; take your inheritance, the kingdom prepared for you since the creation of the world.'" Notice that the blessing of faith given to Abraham (Genesis 15:6) comes as God the Father's free gift, as it is in Ephesians 2:1-10. That faith results in good works from his powerful grace, as Jesus' description says.

On the other hand, the human "goats," who only live for themselves or do good actions for selfish reasons, will receive Jesus' words, "Depart from me, you who are cursed, into the eternal fire prepared for the devil and his angels." They bring God's curse on themselves by their selfish rebellion.

As a result, Jesus' description emphasizes their responsibility by leaving out God's part, unlike the description of the blessing "by my Father" given to the sheep (verse 34). In verse 46, Jesus describes the goats' sad destination as "eternal punishment," whereas "the righteous" will go "to eternal life." Yes, God is just in punishing self-centered sin.

Therefore, the next stage on our journey with Jesus and another shining angle of Jesus' jewel is the public Final Judgment, when the "sheep" will lift up both God's grace in accepting them as believers because of Jesus' perfection and his justice in judging rebellious unbelievers. A number of people have divided this Judgment Day into two judgments, but I don't find that teaching in the Scriptures.

However, it is true that immediately after we die, our souls will appear before God to be sent to heaven or hell until Jesus' public judgment. The writer to the Hebrews, in describing Jesus' sacrifice of himself on the cross, writes, "Just as man was destined to die once, and after that to face judgment, so Christ was sacrificed once to take away the sins of many people; and he will appear a second time, not to bear sin, but to bring salvation to those who are waiting for him" (Hebrews 9:27, 28). Are you eagerly awaiting his coming, when he will publicly declare you as a believer "not guilty"?

God's gift of a new creation as our eternal home

In Revelation 21, John sees a vision of "a new heaven and a new earth, for the first heaven and the first earth had passed away, and there was no longer any sea." A newly-created universe will be a large part of the glittering gem of our inheritance (21:1) toward which we eagerly race. John summarizes a symbolic picture of a new universe that will replace this present cosmos. Again, the word translated "new" is the same one as the one used for the new covenant meaning "new in quality" or "new and improved," not "brand-new." Oh, wouldn't it have been a great joy to get a peek at that symbolic vision with John!

However, John's focus is not on that spectacular new universe but on the bride of the Lamb descending toward the new earth. That sight will be our focus as well. On the other hand, the absence of the sea that surrounds John on the prison Isle of Patmos during God's vision is interesting but mysterious. The sea may be symbolic of the nations' evil systems or the literal oceans' water.

This leg of our journey is an exhilarating one, since the "new and improved" Jerusalem will come down "from God out of heaven" (21:2). I believe that the new Jerusalem's descent to the new earth in Revelation 21 begins where 1 Thessalonians 4:13-18 ends. The new Jerusalem is a figurative picture of all believers in our new resurrection bodies. Having gone up to meet Jesus in the air, we will then return with him to the new earth as the Father's heavenly palace of John 14:1-4. The wedding dress worn by the city is a dead or live give-away that the city actually stands for the old-and-new-covenant people of God as his bride.

In conclusion, the ever-practical Paul in 1 Thessalonians 4:17b, 18 writes, "And so we will be with the Lord forever. Therefore encourage each other with these words." People have assumed that we go off to heaven from the atmosphere, but that passage does not say where we will be with the Lord Jesus.

However, Revelation 21 does. In chapter 22, the new-Jerusalem vision pictures the water of life flowing in a river down the middle of the wide street in the city with the tree of life standing on both sides of the river. Twelve crops a year come from that tree.

This picture is full of symbolism. Jesus promises the Holy Spirit as living water to believers, while the tree of life begins in the Garden of Eden. The scene drips with perfect eternal life as God's gift of grace, since the tree's leaves are for the nations' healing. Our final healing begins after death but will be complete as we live forever in our resurrection bodies on the new earth.

Two more details give us great hope as hurrying travelers. In Revelation 21:22, John says that he doesn't see a temple in the city because God the Father and Jesus are its temple. Since believers are spiritually connected to God through Jesus, we will be connected to him then in all perfection. In 22:5, he observes that "the throne of God and of the Lamb will be in the city, and his servants will serve him. They will see his face, and his name will be on their foreheads." We will see God with our spiritual, new-body eyes!

What a comfort for us who face the uncertainties of old age and death along our life's journey to know the final destination on our pathway, once we trust in the 3-in-1 God who makes it all possible through Jesus Christ!

Bible Discussion Questions:

1. Read Matthew 25:31-46. How can anyone claim that God is not a God of justice in the light of Jesus' words here and elsewhere in the New Testament? What is his basis for judging true believers "not guilty" in verse 34? Why, then, must we do good works in our lives, if they aren't God's reason for giving us his final kingdom? How do you feel about the coming Final Judgment in the light of this passage?

2. In what ways is the picture of the new Jerusalem descending toward the new earth (Revelation 21) different from the way you have thought about what will happen to us after we die? How much do you look forward to that future event? Explain.

* * *

One Step on Our Journey with Jesus: In your prayers, praise God the Father for his perfect justice (his "guilty" verdict) that he gave to Jesus in our place. Praise Jesus for his perfect substitution for us on the cross taking on himself our Father's just anger against our sins. Praise the Holy Spirit for giving us faith and the new birth to live for the one eternal God in his strength, not our own. Praise him as your one true God.

* * *

Why we need to persevere in running God's race

I must make one observation about our journey toward our final inheritance. The question can arise why we need to go on our trip toward our final future if we can never fully receive that amazing gift in this life. Why don't we just receive God's rescue and wait for the next life? Why should we struggle through all of the obstacles in our old age on the road toward final perfection?

First of all, with such an attitude, the people who ask those questions may be fooling themselves into thinking that Jesus has rescued them, when he hasn't. When God gives us the Holy Spirit, he enables us to *want* to learn about him and his Word and *desire* to travel in this life toward our final destination, even though we don't receive it before death or Jesus' return.

Second, God's gift for all true believers is the urgency to run the race. He also gives us the spiritual energy to sustain us during that trip through Jesus' victory by the Holy Spirit's power. We may take an occasional detour, but he will always bring us back to the straight and narrow road toward the new earth.

For example, Paul gives us the example of his own life in Philippians chapter three. Often, Paul writes against the Judaizers, who want Gentile believers to become Jews as a condition for being a church member. He responds to their arguments by telling the Philippians to watch out for those people who want them to fall back into the old covenant (verses 1-3). Then, he describes all of the qualities he previously used to gain God's gratitude, as many people try to do: circumcision, Israelite heritage, strict Phariseeism, persecution of the church, and faultless legalism (Philippians 3:4-6).

However, he confesses, "But whatever was to my profit I now consider loss for the sake of Christ. What is more, I consider everything a loss compared to the surpassing greatness of knowing Christ Jesus my Lord, for whose sake I have lost all things. I consider them rubbish, that I may gain Christ and be found in him, not having a righteousness of my own that comes from the law, but that which comes through faith in Christ—the righteousness that comes from God and is by faith" (Philippians 3:7-9). Paul's past reliance on his heritage and actions to get God's approval is worth about as much as manure ("rubbish").

I once talked with a middle-aged man who had grown up in a Christian home and church in a town that had a lot of Christians. As a result, he assumed like Paul that he was a believer. However, he joined an evangelistic calling-group and discovered that he had never made a personal commitment to Jesus as the only Path to God the Father by the Holy Spirit's power. He had never personally known the one true God of the Bible. As a result of that outreach training, he finally made that commitment to Jesus by God's great grace!

The comfort and hope of our final goal

Furthermore, Paul continues in Philippians chapter three to describe our Christian life as a race. What is his goal at the finish line? In verses 10 and 11, he writes, "I want to know Christ and the power of his resurrection and the fellowship of his sufferings, becoming like him in his death, and so, somehow, to attain to the resurrection from the dead." In this passage, as we have seen in the previous context, Paul in no way says that we race toward that goal with our own strength, nor does he imply that we in any way earn that final goal.

Our final goal at the end of our long path is our future resurrection perfection, all of which will happen to God's complete credit. It is the huge diamond inheritance that comforts and challenges us as we run our race toward God's glorious future.

Paul then qualifies his situation as follows: "Not that I have already obtained all this, or have already been made perfect, but I press on to take hold of that for which Christ Jesus took hold of me.... Forgetting what is behind and straining toward what is ahead, I press on toward the goal to win the prize for which God has called me heavenward in Christ Jesus" (Philippians 3:12-14). If Apostle Paul, who sacrifices his "good" life as a Pharisee to endure hardship and opposition as he preaches the good news about Jesus and establishes many churches, is not yet perfect at this point in his life, I certainly can't claim to be perfect either.

Moreover, Paul borrows the verbs translated "press" and "strain" for running our race toward final perfection from the language of the Olympic Greek games of track and field. However, all true believers will win the competition at the end of our run toward the prize of God's gift of resurrection perfection after death and in the new creation. That struggle is not against other people but, instead, against our sinful natures, the devil, and the world's temptations.

The victorious Greek Olympians received a wreath crown as their prize; but our final inheritance is free, flawless, eternal life with our great God of grace.

May God empower all of us to run the race boldly toward final perfection. God enables us to run toward his free gift of Jesus' final victory. He wants to give us progress on the path that will end in his gift of perfection in the new universe.

How, then, can we be discouraged or only live for selfish satisfaction in our old age?

Bible Discussion Questions:

1. If we can never be perfect in this life, why should we run the race with Paul, according to Philippians chapter three? Read that chapter. What kinds of qualities or actions do people nowadays try to claim as their credit with God the way Paul has previously done?

2. Why does Paul consider "rubbish" his previous claims for credit (verse 8)? What right standing does Paul claim as credit before God the Judge (verse 10)? What biblical events are God's "ticket" to get us into heaven and the new universe? Why?

3. Why do you suppose Paul chose the picture and words of an Olympic race to picture his race toward the final inheritance (verses 12-14)? In your own words, describe the prize that Paul and we are running to get (clues: verses 10-12).

* * *

The Final Step on Our Journey with Jesus: Give up by God's grace your reliance on earthly things and people for satisfaction and meaning. Instead, focus your hope on the God of the Bible so that you can run the race humbly, boldly, and

prayerfully. Ask him to make you his agent of blessing to other people. Pray persistently for his power to persevere on the path toward perfection.

* * *

I hope that God has comforted and challenged you on our joyful journey with Jesus throughout these pages. May the 3-in-1 God bless you with his divine power through Jesus' triumph to enable you to persevere and progress on your trip to our final inheritance in his new creation. See you there! Come soon, Jesus! In his perfect grace, Bruce Leiter.